The Creative Power *of your* Words

Printed in the United States of America
ISBN: 978-1-963964-31-8 (Paperback)
ISBN: 978-1-963964-32-5 (Digital)
Library of Congress Control Number: 2026902753

Published by Cocoon to Wings Publishing
7810 Gall Blvd., #311
Zephyrhills, FL 33541
www.CocoontoWingsBooks.com
(813) 906-WING (9464)

Scriptures marked CEV are taken from Copyright © 1995 by American Bible Society. For more information about CEV, visit www.bibles.com and www.cev.bible.

DR. SHIRLEY GEORGE

The Creative Power *of your* Words

Cocoon to Wings
PUBLISHING

Contents

Dedication

This book is lovingly dedicated to my husband, Kasey, and to my children: Josh, Melanie, Jeff, Jeremy, and Patreese.

"May the words of my mouth and the meditation of my heart be pleasing in Your sight, O Lord, my Rock and my Redeemer."

Advance Praise

The Creative Power of Your Words is a deeply personal and biblically grounded book that reminds us just how much weight our words carry. Dr. Shirley George writes not only from theory, but from a journey marked by pain, healing, and redemption, showing how God's Word has the power to restore what trauma, fear, and false beliefs have tried to steal. With honesty, compassion, and strong scriptural foundation, she calls readers to align their thoughts and declarations with the truth of Christ and the authority He has given us. This book will encourage, challenge, and equip anyone who is ready to break free from old narratives and begin speaking life, faith, and healing over their future. "

– Dr. Brent Simpson
Lead Pastor of ARISE Church

The Creative Power of Your Words by Dr. Shirley George is a profound and timely reminder that our words are never empty - they carry spiritual authority and real impact in the physical realm. This book beautifully unpacks the divine principle that spoken words shape atmospheres, influence outcomes, and release either life or limitation. With spiritual depth and practical insight, Dr. Shirley reveals how the unseen spiritual dimension responds to what we speak. This is not just a book to read, but a truth to live by. Powerful, revelatory, and transformative - this book will change the way you speak, pray, and live.

- Pastor George Mathew
President, George Mathew Ministries

It is a profound honor and joy to see *The Creative Power of Your Words: Minding What Holds the Power to Shape Your Destiny* come to life. I have had the privilege of knowing Dr. Shirley George for more than 10 years. I can say with certainty that she is not only a gifted author but a true woman of God who fully embodies the message of this book.

I am so excited for the world to experience this life-changing book, which will expose the enemy's lies and reveal God's truth in many lives. Dr. Shirley's journey from the brokenness of her past to a life of healing and transformation is an enlightening testimony of what can happen when our words align with God's truth.

I pray that this book would inspire every reader to guard their hearts and understand that our words are like seeds that can cultivate a destiny filled with God's promises. I am confident that as you read this book, you will be empowered to speak life, blessing, and victory into every area of your life.

- Dr. Ashley Prathyash & Pastor Prathyash Thomas
Hope to the Nations International Ministry

Understanding the words you speak either acquit or condemn you when you stand before God (Matthew 12:37) makes this book a critical key to unlock your victory. In *The Creative Power of Your Words,* Dr. Shirley George gives the reader a war strategy to take back what the enemy has stolen through our verbal agreements. Shirley uses personal experiences and testimonies of others to bring a fresh revelation on how to regain control of your tongue. Each chapter concludes with an activation to help you recognize where your words need to change from death to life. This book is a wonderful tool to help you accelerate into your destiny. Thank you, Shirley, for your obedience, clarity and wisdom to help so many find their voice. The best is yet to come!

- Phyllis Tarbox Ph.D.

Vice President of Above & Beyond Christian Counseling

Foreword

There are books that inform, books that inspire, and books that quietly accompany us through the valleys of life. But every so often, a book emerges that does something far more profound—it awakens us. *The Creative Power of Your Words* is one of those rare works.

Dr. Shirley George writes not as a distant observer of pain but as someone who has walked through the fire and emerged with a testimony forged in truth. Her story is not merely a narrative of survival; it is a living demonstration of the spiritual principle she teaches: **words shape destinies**. With honesty, courage, and deep biblical insight, she invites readers to examine the unseen forces that have influenced their lives; forces often carried on the wings of spoken words.

From the opening chapter, Dr. George reminds us that creation itself began with a voice. God spoke, and the universe responded. That same divine pattern continues in us, His image-bearers. Our words carry weight, authority, and spiritual resonance. They can build or break, heal or wound, bless or curse. Many people know this in theory;

few understand it in the marrow of their being. Dr. George is one of the few.

Her journey, from childhood trauma, fear, and emotional bondage to healing, identity, and spiritual authority, is woven throughout these pages with remarkable vulnerability. She does not shy away from the darkness she endured, yet she never glorifies it. Instead, she magnifies the God who redeems, restores, and rewrites stories through the power of His Word spoken in faith.

This book is not simply about positive thinking or motivational speech. It is about aligning our words with the eternal truth of Scripture. It is about reclaiming the authority Christ has already given us. It is about choosing life, intentionally, consistently, and courageously.

As you turn these pages, you will find yourself challenged, encouraged, and empowered. You will see your own story reflected in unexpected ways. And you may discover, perhaps for the first time, that the words you speak today are shaping the life you will live tomorrow.

Dr. George's message is timely, necessary, and deeply anointed. My prayer is that as you read, you will not only understand the creative power of your words, but you will also begin to use that power to build the life God intended for you all along.

May this book be a catalyst for healing, a spark for renewed faith, and a reminder that your voice carries the echo of the One who spoke light into darkness.

Choose your words wisely. Speak them boldly. And watch God transform your world.

Dr. Lucille Murray, PhD, MSN/Ed., RN

Preface

Every book has a beginning, but this one was birthed from a place much deeper than inspiration. It was born from a lifetime of wrestling with words, words spoken over me, words spoken against me, and eventually, words spoken through me by the Spirit of God.

For years, I lived under the weight of negative declarations that shaped my identity and clouded my destiny. I carried wounds from childhood, fear from adolescence, and guilt from adulthood. I believed the lies spoken by others and repeated them to myself until they became the soundtrack of my life.

But God, in His mercy, interrupted that cycle.

Through Scripture, through healing, and through the gentle voice of the Holy Spirit, I discovered a truth that changed everything: **words are spiritual containers of power**. They can imprison or liberate, destroy or restore, curse or bless. And when aligned with God's Word, they carry the authority of heaven itself.

This book is the result of that revelation. It is my testimony, my journey, and my offering to anyone who has ever felt silenced, broken, or bound by the words of others. My prayer is that as you read, you will not only understand the creative power of your words, but you will also begin to use them with intention, faith, and authority.

May these pages lead you into freedom, healing, and a renewed understanding of who you are in Christ.

Acknowledgements

I wish to express my deepest gratitude to my husband for his unwavering support, encouragement, and patience throughout this journey.

My sincere appreciation goes to my publisher, Stephanie Outten, and to the entire dedicated team at Cocoon to Wings Publishing for their creativity, professionalism, and meticulous attention to detail. Your words of encouragement and faithful prayers during my physical challenges played a vital role in bringing this book to life.

I am also deeply thankful to Pastor Tina Blount, Pastor George Mathew, Dr. Ashley, Pastor Prathyash, and Dr. Brent Simpson for their continual reminders, guidance, and encouragement.

To my sisters-in-law, Celine Chacko and Alice Abraham, thank you for your steadfast support and prayers.

Finally, I extend heartfelt thanks to my children for their incredible support and for sharing their talents in the creation of the book cover.

Introduction

Words are everywhere. They fill our conversations, shape our thoughts, and influence our emotions. Yet most people never stop to consider the spiritual force behind them. We speak casually, reactively, and often carelessly; never realizing that our words are seeds, and every seed produces a harvest.

This book is an invitation to pause and examine the words you speak, and the words spoken over you. It is a journey into Scripture, science, personal testimony, and spiritual truth. You will discover:

- Why God created the world through speech

- How your thoughts become words, and your words become reality

- How negative declarations open doors to fear, anxiety, and bondage

- How faith-filled words activate God's promises

- How to reclaim your authority in Christ

- How to speak blessings over your life, family, and future

This is not a book about positive thinking. It is a book about **biblical truth, spiritual authority,** and **the supernatural power of the spoken word**.

As you read, I encourage you to do more than absorb information. Speak the Scriptures aloud. Declare God's promises. Break agreement with lies. And watch as the atmosphere of your life begins to shift.

Your words matter. Your voice matters. And your breakthrough may be one declaration away.

CHAPTER 1

The Creative Power of the Spoken Word

In the beginning, before sound, before form, before time itself, there was only silence and darkness. The earth was formless and void; the deep waters stirred beneath the weight of nothingness. Yet even in that silence, something waited. The Spirit of God hovered alive, aware, ready to speak.

Then it happened.

The first sound in all of creation.

A voice.

> "And God said, 'Let there be light,' and there was light." – Genesis 1:3 (NIV)

With that single declaration, eternity split open. Light shattered the darkness. Chaos bent into order. What had never been suddenly was.

Genesis doesn't describe gradual unfolding; it reveals a series of divine commands, each word bursting with purpose and power. **"And God said..."** Again and again, creation answered. Stars ignited. Oceans formed. Life awakened.

God's spoken word is the fundamental creative force, the energy of divine creation, the current that moves all things into being. His voice does not describe reality; it defines it. It is the energy that calls matter into motion, which turns silence into sound and emptiness into form.

As Scripture declares, God **"calls into being things that were not."** - Romans 4:17 (NIV) Through His Word, all things came to exist, and through that same Word, all things are sustained. **The Son is the radiance of God's glory and exact representation of His being, sustaining all things by His powerful word.** - Hebrews 1:3 (NIV)

That voice, the original vibration of creation, still echoes through the universe. It is the heartbeat of existence, the living frequency that brings light into darkness and order into chaos.

This is the mystery and the power of the spoken word. When God speaks, worlds are born. And when we, made in His image, learn the power of our own words, we begin to understand what it means to create with them.

The same divine principle that spoke the universe into existence still flows through the breath of humanity. When God created humankind, He didn't merely form us from dust. He breathed into us the breath of life. That breath carried His essence, His Spirit, and with it, His creative power.

We are the only beings made in His image, and with that image came the gift of speech, the ability to shape reality with words. Our voices carry echoes of that first divine command. What we speak has weight. It vibrates through the atmosphere, setting things in motion, influencing hearts, shifting possibilities, building, or breaking what surrounds us.

Words are not just sounds. They are containers of energy, vessels of intention, infused with life or death, faith or fear, truth or deception. The same principle that spoke galaxies into being now rests on our lips.

Every time we speak, we participate, whether knowingly or not, in the same creative rhythm that began in Genesis. God spoke, and reality responded. We speak, and the world around us still responds.

In the Garden of Eden, Satan came to Eve in the form of a serpent, using clever and deceptive words to twist what God had said. God clearly told Adam not to eat from the tree of the knowledge of good and evil, warning that if they did, they would surely die. But Satan, in Genesis 3:1(NIV), challenged God's word by planting doubt in Eve's mind. He asked, **"Did God really say you must not eat from any tree in the garden?"** Then he boldly lied and said, **"You will not certainly die. For God knows that when you eat from it your eyes will be opened, and you will be like God, knowing good and evil."** Genesis 3:4-5 (NIV). His words were smooth and tricky, designed to confuse and deceive. Instead of trusting God's truth, Eve listened to the serpent's lies, and the power of those twisted words led her to take the fruit and eat it. That one act changed everything. It shows us how powerful words can be, especially when they are used to twist the truth and lead people away from God's will.

Have you ever felt stuck in the pain of your past when life becomes hard? In those moments, your inner voice may start to question everything, your worth and your purpose, while others around you seem happy and full of joy. It feels like a painful return to a lonely childhood, a deep place where no one sees your pain or hears your cries.

Even when you're with people, this inner fight can feel like a storm of bad thoughts, sadness, and even hate. You may hear words like, "You're useless, can't do anything right," or "You're a failure and a shame to us." These words aren't just sounds; they are sharp arrows that hit your heart, leaving you empty and hopeless.

As Robert Fulghum, an American writer, penned, **"Sticks and stones may break our bones, but words will break our hearts."** His words help us see how powerful speech can be in shaping how we feel and live.

It's like you start building walls inside to keep yourself safe, but they only make your mind feel like a war zone filled with dark thoughts. This struggle tells you that no one cares, not even God, and that anything good you try will fail. Words are deeply powerful, and in your weakest times, they can feel like weapons aimed at your heart and soul.

I went through deep pain during my childhood. That pain followed me into my adult life. When I was growing up, my siblings and I lived with our aunt and uncle. But it was not a loving or safe home. It was a place full of harsh words and silent anger. Aunt Mary often used hurtful words, especially toward me, the oldest. She also criticized our parents, who worked abroad. The house was filled with negativity. Joy felt like a thing from the past.

Aunt Mary tightly controlled our lives. We had no freedom to enjoy the little things of childhood. We were always trying to be accepted and feel loved. We were not allowed to spend time with friends; they were not part of our world, not even during holidays. After school, we had to help with chores. We helped cook, clean, and wash dishes. Fun and play were replaced with work and stress. Being away from my parents made me feel alone, angry, and deeply sad. I missed them all the time. I would sit and stare out the window, as tears would roll down my face.

My aunt would shout, "Why are you crying like you lost your husband?" I was only nine years old. Her harsh words hurt me deeply, damaging my self-worth.

I started experiencing chest pains and a racing heart. My aunt said God was punishing me and teaching me a lesson. Growing up, I was taught that getting sick was a form of punishment from God, a way for Him to correct me. She reinforced this belief, telling me I was disrespectful and disobedient for staying up late to do my homework, despite her rule to be in bed by 9:00 p.m. These experiences gave me a terribly distorted view of who God was. I came to believe that God was angry with me and that I could never live up to His expectations. Every time I fell ill, I was convinced it was my punishment. I was trapped in a cycle of guilt, shame, and condemnation, filled with self-pity and self-hatred. It was a heavy burden to carry. Sometimes, I would pull out my hair to ease the pain of shame and condemnation in my heart.

Growing up, my aunt often silenced my voice, and as a result, I became afraid to express my feelings in front of others. When I was eleven years old, we were on our way to a wedding with my cousins and their parents. I ended up sitting beside the taxi driver. During that ride, an unwanted incident occurred, one that left an unforgettable scar. Each time he turned or twisted the wheel, his elbow pressed against my chest. I was already struggling with changes happening to my body. In that moment, I felt frozen, unable to speak or express the pain I was enduring. I kept that and his touches as I got out of his car, all buried inside.

One of my older cousins, who visited us often, liked to scare me with horror stories. She warned that men could sneak into my room at night and hurt me. She said they could hide under the bed. "Make sure your windows are closed," she'd whisper. "Check your room before sleeping." Her words planted fear in me.

I used to take public transportation to high school. The bus wasn't just crowded; it was suffocating. Bodies would press against mine, a buzzing, stinging invasion that made my skin crawl. That feeling of being swarmed by bees mirrored the choking fear and raw anxiety that consumed me during every agonizing ride. I began to believe that *all* men wanted to harm me. I feared every man in my neighborhood, at school, and even in college.

When I saw a man, I would run. I thought that was the only way to stay safe. In nursing school, we had to visit hospitals as part of our training. I would avoid any male doctor or worker who came near. I feared men, darkness, and the unknown. My cousin's horror stories trapped me in a shadowed world. A tiny sound at night would jolt me out of bed, convinced someone had broken in. Words are like seeds. A seed of fear was planted in me through words. That seed grew into a large tree. It bore fruit, fear, worry, and anxiety.

After graduating from high school, I entered the College of Nursing with both hope and uncertainty. During that season, an evangelist lovingly shared the gospel with me. I repented of my sins and received Jesus as my Savior. Embracing my identity as a child of God stirred within me the courage to face life's struggles.

> "The Lord is on my side; I will not fear. What can man do to me?" Psalm 118:6 (NKJV).

Whenever challenges rose against me, I whispered, "The Lord is on my side." I also held tightly to the promise in Deuteronomy 31:8 (NIV): **"The Lord Himself goes before**

you and He will be with you; He will never leave you nor forsake you. Do not be afraid; do not be discouraged." Each time I spoke that verse, courage and boldness lifted my spirit, reminding me that the Lord stands beside me and I am never alone.

After graduating as a registered nurse, my best friend introduced me to her brother-in-law. I trusted her deeply, as if she were my own sister. And I had begun to trust God more fully, even with the trauma around men. Her brother-in-law and I spent several months learning each other's hearts through long-distance calls, and before long, I felt safe enough to marry him. I entered the marriage believing my husband would be a place of safety, shielding me from other men, and he was. God later blessed us with three beautiful sons. After a few years of our marriage, I became overwhelmed with the challenges of life. To say that my life was *full* is an understatement. As a psychiatric nurse, a wife, a mother of three children, and a caregiver for two elderly parents, I found it nearly impossible to get anything done. I would start cooking, but then abandon it to sort laundry, only to leave that mid-task to go grocery shopping and then pick up kids from school. By the end of the day, I would find I hadn't completed any of my chores.

My mind was a battlefield of negative thoughts rooted in my childhood. When I didn't meet my own standards, I felt incredibly guilty and would condemn myself by repeating the words my aunt used to say about me: "I am useless, I am slow, and disorganized." I carried the guilt of feeling that I was never good enough as a mother or as a wife and that God was angry with me. My guilt was that I was not able to complete any task on time. Words spoken over you can truly shape what you think. If those words are harsh, they can produce deep emotional pain of guilt, condemnation, fear, and anxiety in you.

I was trapped in a deep rut, my spirit heavy and my path unclear. I prayed with all my heart for God to show me a way out. And just when I felt I couldn't bear the weight anymore, I began searching for Christian counseling on my computer. That's when I stumbled upon a seminar titled **"Released to Soar,"** by **Above and Beyond Christian Counseling**. I attended the three-day seminar, which dramatically shifted my perspective. It unveiled the concept of "word curses" (words spoken over you negatively), revealing how they can open the door for the enemy to wreak havoc in our lives. I learned how words can impact a person. They can either build you up or destroy you. This profound realization came after I understood that Jesus had already paid the ultimate price for my sins and sickness on the Cross. That lifted the immense burden of guilt and condemnation I had carried through the negative words spoken over my life. That day was a moment of true liberation, one that touched the deepest part of my soul. It allowed me to forgive my aunt from the depths of my heart and finally let go of all the judgment against her and my cousin.

I embraced my identity and my authority in Christ Jesus. I boldly began to declare scriptures like, "I am a child of

God, and I am forgiven. If the Son sets you free, you are free indeed. I am greatly blessed, deeply loved, and highly favored by God. I can do all things through Christ Jesus who strengthens me." These scriptures became my daily confession. Romans 10:17 (NKJV) says, **"So then faith comes by hearing, and hearing by the word of God."** The emotional pain vanished, and the self-pity parties ceased. I was filled with boldness and courage. Praise God! He can pull out those weeds and plant truth instead. His Word brings healing and new life.

My journey from brokenness to healing vividly illustrates the power of spoken words, both those directed at us by others and those we speak to ourselves. It showcases the incredible potential for change when we replace negative self-talk with affirmations of faith and truth.

The Creative Power of Your Words

Have you ever stopped to think about how powerful your words actually are?

The Bible says in Proverbs 18:21 (NKJV), **"Death and life are in the power of the tongue, And those who love it will eat its fruit."** That means of the thousands of words you speak every day, each one can help shape your life or hinder it.

In Genesis 1:3 (NIV), when God saw the darkness, He didn't say how bad it was. Instead, He said, **"Let there be light,"** and light appeared. God entrusted Adam and Eve with authority over the earth. He commanded them to be fruitful, to multiply, and to rule. But when they listened to the lies of the enemy, Satan, they surrendered that divine authority. This moment reveals just how powerful and dangerous words can be.

The words we speak and the words we choose to believe carry immense weight. Every time we open our mouths, we are aligning ourselves with either the voice of God or the voice of the enemy. That's why it's so important to speak with wisdom, care, and conviction.

Scripture reminds us in Job 22:28 (NKJV):

> "You will also decree a thing, and it will be established for you; so light will shine on your ways."

So, speak with intention and purpose.

1. Anchor Your Words in God's Word: Why it matters: Faith comes by hearing the Word of God (Romans 10:17). When your words agree with Scripture, they carry divine authority. Find verses that speak to your situation (e.g., peace, provision, healing).

   Declare them aloud daily.

   Personalize them: "The Lord is my Shepherd; I lack nothing."

2. Guard the Gate of Your Mouth: Why it matters: Purposeful speech requires discipline. Idle or negative words weaken spiritual authority.

Ask the Holy Spirit to "set a guard over your mouth." (Psalm 141:3).

When you catch yourself speaking doubt, stop and reframe the statement in faith.

Surround yourself with people who speak life.

Speak with faith.

3. See Before You Say: Faith speaks what it sees in the Spirit, even before it manifests in the natural.

    Visualize the promise fulfilled, see the healing, the restoration, the breakthrough.

If you are struggling, tape the promises to different places in your home, office, or car, and read them aloud until they become your language. Prepare your faith language like you would learn Italian for a trip to Italy. Speak as if it's already done: "Thank You, Lord, that it is finished." This is the language of God. This is the vibration of creation. Speak as one who carries the authority of heaven because your words truly matter.

Reclaiming Your Authority in Christ

Are you still letting the enemy control parts of your life?
Jesus already won the battle on the Cross. He said in John 19:30 (NIV), **"It is finished."** That means the power of sin, sickness, and fear is broken. He gave us authority. We need to walk in it.

Sometimes we say things like, "I'm sick, I am tired," or "I'll never change." But the Word of God says something different. Isaiah 53:5 (NKJV) says, **"By His stripes, we are healed."** When we agree with God's Word and speak it, we release healing power into our lives.

One day, I started having a terrible toothache. I knew I would need a root canal on that tooth. It was the weekend, and the pain was unbearable. I started to panic. But then I stopped and rebuked the fear in Jesus' name. I began declaring healing over my tooth. I said, "Lord Jesus, thank You for doing the root canal and stopping the pain." Right away, the pain disappeared.

Look at James 4:7 (NIV): **"Submit yourselves, then, to God. Resist the devil, and he will flee from you."** This verse is clear. If we want to walk in faith, we must first submit to God and His Word. That means we read it, believe it, and speak it aloud with faith. The Word of God is more than a book. It's a weapon.

Luke 10:19 (NIV) is another promise: **"I have given you authority to trample on snakes and scorpions and to overcome all the power of the enemy; nothing will harm you."** This is not just a nice idea, it's the truth. When you believe it and speak it, nothing the enemy throws at you can destroy you.

We must *speak up*. Declare God's promises audibly over your life. Say aloud, "I am the righteousness of God in Christ." Remind the devil that he has no power over you.

Don't let fear, guilt, or lies rule your mind. Jesus already won the victory; you need to live in it.

Before we speak, we should always check the root of our thoughts. If our words don't line up with God's truth, they might come from the enemy. And once we release them by speaking, they gain power. That's why it's important to be careful. God gave man dominion over His creation, which is to be exercised through the use of His words. We can bring breakthroughs and transformation to our lives by declaring God's promises. We have been given His power to create life. We must use it with wisdom and faith.

A Personal Journey of Healing Through Words

In 2001, my life changed, painfully and frighteningly. Stress and constant negativity had worn me down so badly that I ended up in and out of the hospital with chest pain and palpitations for three long months. I was weak and scared. I worried I might die and leave my young children without a mom. My anxiety was overwhelming. I couldn't even lift a cup of coffee without help. I kept imagining myself lying in a casket, gone too soon.

In my lowest moment, I cried out to God, asking Him to heal me. In desperation, I made a promise: "Lord, if You show me a Bible verse for healing, I will stop taking my medication (which had no effect on me) and instead trust in Your Word." With shaky hands, I opened the Bible, and there it was.

> **"My child, pay attention to what I say. Listen carefully to my words. Don't lose sight of them. Let them penetrate deep into your heart, for they bring life to those who find them, and healing to their whole body. Guard your heart above all else, for it determines the course of your life. Avoid all perverse talk; stay away from corrupt speech" Proverbs 4:20–24 (NLT).**

Those verses hit me like a bolt of light. God had answered my prayer. I felt His presence, love, and gentle voice saying, "I hear you." Before that moment, I hadn't realized how often I spoke fear and defeat over myself. But I accepted the truth that day, God listens, even to the silent whispers we tell ourselves. I made a bold and personal decision. I stopped taking medicine and began declaring healing scriptures instead. **"By His stripes you have been healed"** 1 Peter 2:24b (NIV).

Please understand, I'm not telling anyone to stop their medication. My choice was an act of my faith, born from desperation. And God met me right there. Just like someone takes medicine three times a day, I read and spoke healing scriptures morning, noon, and night. Slowly, my strength returned. I got better. God honored His Word.

Those scriptures became my lifeline. Trusting Scripture instead of medicine wasn't easy. I battled fear and unbelief every day. But I clung to the promises in God's Word. I believed that if He said I was healed, then healing was coming. My faith was tested, but the Word gave me peace. It gave me hope. And step by step, it brought healing.

Think about this verse:

> **1 Peter 3:10 (NIV): "For whoever would love life and see good days must keep their tongue from evil and their lips from deceitful speech."**

Your life today is shaped by the words you've spoken over the years. Every time you speak, you are planting something. Have you ever tried positive affirmations? Try saying, *"I am highly favored, greatly blessed, and deeply loved by God. I have authority in Christ Jesus. I can do all things through Him who gives me strength."* These kinds of words can light up your life with hope, joy, and strength. Proverbs 16:24 (NIV) says, **"Gracious words are a honeycomb, sweet to the soul and healing to the bones."**

Now, flip the script. Have you ever caught yourself muttering, "I can't do this. I'm a burden on others. I'm just a flop?" These negative words can also take root and grow into fear, sadness, insecurity, or discouragement.

The Enduring Influence of Words:
A Client's Story

Words have a lasting impact. They can shape how we see ourselves and how we live. A client shared with me a painful memory from her childhood. Her brother repeatedly called her a lesbian, even though she was a child and did not understand the term at the time. The incessant repetition, however, gradually began to affect her internal world, her thoughts, and emotions. Those words slowly eroded her identity and self-perception, creating internal confusion that contributed to the development of same sex attraction. It wasn't something she sought out; it was something spoken over her repeatedly.

Even though she went to church for healing from this bondage, her friends and family members began to pull away. She felt rejected and completely alone. She grew angry with herself and with her brother. Over time, her hurt turned into depression, and she needed medication to cope. That's when she decided to seek professional counseling.

Her healing journey truly began during counseling and through a powerful experience with a deliverance ministry at Above and Beyond Christian Counseling, a ministry focused on setting people free from their demonic oppressions and the influences of fear, anxiety, depression, or anger. She refused to listen to the enemy's lies and began speaking God's promises over her life. Little by little, the chains from her past began to break. Using God's Word, she declared truth, peace, and hope into her life. Lies were replaced with faith-filled words. Her story became a powerful testimony, a living example of how the Word of God, spoken in faith and with His authority, can bring deep healing and transformation. From a place of darkness and confusion, she stepped into light, wholeness, and purpose.

Another woman, a theology graduate, also encountered the power of words, but in a vastly different way. She felt called to preach, yet fear and anxiety continually held her back. Her husband had spoken harsh, discouraging words to her for years. Those words filled her with fear and insecurity, which made her feel unworthy to stand before people. One day, she was invited to preach at a church. But when she stepped up to the podium, she realized she couldn't open her mouth because the fear was overwhelming. She felt as if she were melting like snow before the congregation. In desperation, she came to me for help.

Through counseling, she slowly rediscovered her voice. She realized that just as negative words had chained her, positive, faith-filled words could finally set her free. She began to push through the dirt and mud her husband had tried to bury her under. She would declare that her voice carried purpose as she shoveled heavy dirt away. She would declare that God had a great plan and purpose for her life, clearing even more dirt from her soul. Over time, her fear gave way to genuine confidence.

Today, she boldly preaches the gospel in different countries around the world. Her life stands as a radiant testimony to how speaking God's truth can awaken our purpose and release the courage hidden within us.

These two stories remind us how words can be either uplifting or discouraging. When we speak truth, love, and faith, lives change. When we speak what God says, the atmosphere shifts. What was once a story of pain becomes a story of victory. As Proverbs 18:20 (NKJV) says, **"A man's stomach shall be satisfied from the fruit of his mouth; from the harvest of his lips, he shall be filled."**

Your words have power. They can heal, bless, and restore. Choose them wisely and watch what God can do through you.

The Science of Words:
Dr. Masaru Emoto's Water Experiment

Dr. Masaru Emoto, a Japanese scientist, demonstrated how powerful words can be through an experiment with water. He took water samples and spoke aloud to them. To one sample, he spoke with kindness, using words like "You are beautiful" and "amazing." To another, he spoke with anger, saying things like "I hate you" and "You disgust me." After that, he froze the water and took pictures of the crystals.

What he saw was shocking. The water that heard kind words formed beautiful, clear crystals. But the water that heard mean words turned into messy, ugly, broken, and not fully formed shapes.

Our bodies are made of about 60% water! Dr. Emoto's study proves that the words we speak affect us more than we think. Words carry energy, and they can change even water. Speaking kind words can help us feel more peaceful and joyful, while hurtful words can bring confusion and pain. So, the next time you speak, think about the ripples and forms those words might be creating in the water that makes up a significant part of who you are.

The Divine Power of God's Word

Think about how rain and snow fall from the sky, soaking the ground and helping plants grow. In the same way, the words that come from God's mouth are not empty talk. They are full of purpose. God's Word always does what He sends it to do. It never comes back without completing His plan. This is not just nature at work; it's a spiritual truth.

> **"As the rain and the snow come down from heaven, and do not return to it without watering the earth and making it bud and flourish, so that it yields seed for the sower and bread for the eater, so is My word that goes out from My mouth: It will not return to me empty, but will accomplish what I desire and achieve the purpose for which I sent it." Isaiah 55:10-11(NIV)**

Markus Zusak, author of *The Book Thief,* wrote, *"Words are singularly the most powerful force available to humanity. Words have energy and power with the ability to help, to heal, to hinder, to hurt, to harm, to humiliate and to humble."* That's powerful. Think about your own words. Are they building a bright future or bringing darkness and pain?

Look at what God says in Deuteronomy 30:19 (NLT): **"Today I have given you the choice between life and death, between blessings and curses. Now I call on heaven and earth to witness the choice you make. Oh, that you would choose life, so that you and your descendants might live."** This is a profound moment. Heaven and earth are witnesses to your choices. God gives you the freedom to choose life or death, blessing or curse. That choice is yours. The enemy cannot take it from you unless you give it away. God is saying clearly, **"Choose life."** Our words are powerful. As Matthew 12:37 (NKJV) tells us, every word we say will be judged. **"For by your words you will be justified, and by your words you will be condemned."** That's a severe warning.

Even when life is hard, if we think about God's Word and speak it in faith, we line up with His truth. Jesus taught us that our words show what's in our hearts, and we will answer for them. If we keep speaking life, blessings, and truth, we can overcome struggles and walk in all that God has planned for us.

Be careful with your words. Rachel Wolchin, American Author, wrote, *"Be mindful when it comes to your words. A string of some that don't mean much to you may stick with someone else for a lifetime."*

The words we choose to speak are pivotal. They have the potential to mold our lives and leave a lasting impact on those around us. Opting to speak life, blessings, and God's truth over our situations can lead to a profound transformation and fulfillment in our journey of faith.

Reflection Questions:

1. What seeds are you planting?

2. What blessings from Scripture can you start declaring daily to counter old lies?

3. What fearful phrases do you need to stop saying? What faith-filled truths can you replace them with?

4. Is there someone you need to forgive today so that healing can begin?

5. What Scripture will you choose today to declare over your life until it becomes your reality?

Closing Prayer:

Heavenly Father,

Thank You for the truth and power of Your Word. Thank You for showing us that our words carry weight, to heal or to harm, to bless or to break. As we reflect on the pain of the past and the healing You've brought, we are humbled by Your mercy and grace.

Lord, help us to guard our tongues and speak life. Teach us to align our words with Your truth, and to reject every lie the enemy has planted. Heal the wounds caused by harsh words, and replace them with Your promises of love, peace, and restoration.

Thank You for the testimony of transformation, for freedom found through forgiveness, and for the joy that comes when we declare Your Word over our lives. May every seed we plant with our lips bear fruit for Your glory.

In Jesus' powerful name,
Amen.

CHAPTER 2

Words From Your Mouth Begin With Your Thoughts

"What feeds your mind, will lead your life." – Kemi Sogunle, Life Coach and Author.

Think of your mind like a supercomputer, powerful and always working. Like a computer follows its programming, your mind collects information, stores it, and uses it to help you decide what to say and do. Every thought you think is like a piece of code being written inside of you. And those thoughts eventually come out as words.

Now take a moment to consider this: what happens when your mind is full of negative thoughts? It's like having a storm cloud over your day. You might start thinking things like:

1. "I'm not smart enough to understand this material."
2. "Nothing ever works for me."
3. "I feel tired and useless."
4. "I can't do anything right today."
5. "I won't forgive him for what he said."

When these thoughts play repeatedly, they shape how you feel, how you talk, and how you live.

Your Mind Never Stops Thinking

Did you know that scientists from the National Science Foundation say we have between 12,000 and 60,000 thoughts each day? That's a lot of thoughts! Even more surprising, about 80% of them are negative, and 95% are the same thoughts we had yesterday. This means most of us are thinking the same things over and over, and many of those thoughts are not helpful.

Luke 6:45 (NLT) says, **"A good person produces good things from the treasury of a good heart, and an evil person produces evil things from the treasury of an evil heart. What you say flows from what is in your heart."**

That's why it's so important to pay attention to what you're thinking. Thoughts are like seeds, and the words you speak are the plants that grow from them. If your thoughts are kind, loving, and full of faith, your words will reflect that and bless others. But if your thoughts are filled with fear, unforgiveness, or anger, your words will reveal that too.

When my family lived in Philadelphia, my younger son was accidentally left alone on the school bus. Due to a heavy snowstorm, the school closed early. My older son, who was with him, got off the bus thinking his little brother was right behind him. But once he stepped off, he realized his brother hadn't followed. The bus driver continued dropping off the other kids and was heading to park the bus.

When I saw my older son come home without his brother, I panicked. My thoughts immediately went to a dark place. I began saying things like, "Will I ever see my son again?" and "He might not survive out there in this freezing weather." I called everywhere, but no one answered. Most people had already left early because of the storm. Fear gripped my heart, and the things I said were full of hopelessness and despair. I couldn't stop crying and pleading with God to help me find my son. Right before the driver left the bus lot, he checked the bus one last time. That's when he found my son sleeping in his seat. He gently woke him up and brought him safely home. Praise God!

It took me a couple of days to recover from the shock and fear of almost losing my son. If you remember from Chapter 1, I shared how fear and anxiety have been a struggle for me since childhood. Luke 6:45b (ESV) says, **"...For out of the abundance of the heart his mouth speaks."** Out of the fear and worry in my heart, I spoke words of fear and even death.

There was another time when my other son, now grown and married, lost his dog, Smokey, while visiting us. Somehow, Smokey had slipped out of the house. We drove around the neighborhood looking for him. But this time, I didn't panic. My mind was calm and peaceful. I spoke words of faith. I declared, "Smokey will come back." I prayed and asked the Lord to send an angel to bring the dog home.

Sure enough, a little while later, a black SUV pulled into our driveway. A young woman stepped out and asked, "Did you lose a dog?" I said, "Yes! A black Labrador!" I thanked her and told her, "You are an angel sent by God."

Where Do Our Thoughts Come From?

Let's go back to the computer example. When you first buy a computer, it comes only with basic programs or systems. It needs someone to install things outside of the operating system. In the same way, our minds start off ready to learn. Our parents, teachers, friends, and others help shape the way we think by what they say and do.

If you grew up hearing kind words like "You are important," "You are beautiful," or "God made you for a purpose," those thoughts help build confidence. But if you hear painful words like "You'll never be anything in life" or "You're a failure," they can create fear, doubt, and sadness in your heart.

God's Voice Was the First Voice

In Genesis, we learn that God created Adam and Eve in His image. In His likeness, He fashioned them and blessed them. The **first voice** they **heard** from God **was words of blessings**. Genesis 1:28 (NIV) says, **"God blessed them and said to them, 'Be fruitful and increase in number; fill the earth and subdue it. Rule over the fish in the sea and the birds in the sky and over every living creature that moves on the ground.'"** Things were going well for them. God Himself would visit them in the cool of the day. Imagine the profound, breathtaking fellowship between the Creator and the very beings formed in His image and likeness. You can almost see Adam and Eve eagerly awaiting those gentle moments, looking forward to the sacred time when their Maker would walk with them, rejoice with them, and delight in all that had been accomplished. In that original state, everything was perfect, whole, pure, and good.

But this beautiful communion was shattered the moment they listened to another **voice**, the quiet, deceptive whisper of the serpent. Genesis 3:4-5 (NIV) says, **"'You will not certainly die,' the serpent said to the woman. 'For God knows that when you eat from it your eyes will be opened, and you will be like God, knowing good and evil.'"** That voice was full of lies and deception. Eve fell for his deception. When they believed the lie and ate the forbidden fruit, sin entered the world.

This story teaches us something significant: not every **voice** we hear is telling the truth. We must be wise about which voice we choose to follow. Paul says in 2 Corinthians 11:3 (NIV), **"But I am afraid that just as Eve was deceived**

by the serpent's cunning, your minds may somehow be led astray from your sincere and pure devotion to Christ."

Three Voices That Speak into Your Life

Three main voices try to guide your thoughts every day:

1. Your Own Inner Voice

This is the voice within that is shaped by your past, your family, your friends, and what you've been through in life. If you've heard loving, encouraging words, your inner voice is probably kind and pleasant. But if you've faced hurt and rejection, it might be filled with fear, doubt, or shame. This voice affects how you see yourself and how you respond or react to others.

2. The Voice of the Enemy

Satan is a liar who wants to steal your peace and destroy your purpose. We see in 1 Peter 5:8 (NIV), **"Be alert and of sober mind. Your enemy, the devil, prowls around like a roaring lion looking for someone to devour."** Be careful, your enemy, the devil, is always looking for someone to attack. He whispers lies like, "You're worthless," or "God doesn't care about you." These lies are traps meant to bring fear, insecurity, and worry. They can stop you from moving forward.

As Paul warned before, just like Eve was tricked, we can be led away from our strong faith in Christ if we don't stay focused on the truth.

3. God's Voice

God's voice is always filled with love and truth. It is sweet, gentle, and kind. Jesus said in John 10:27 (NIV), **"My sheep listen to My voice; I know them, and they follow Me."** God speaks to us through the Bible, through prayer, and through the Holy Spirit. His voice brings peace, guidance, and clarity. While He may correct us when we go astray, He never brings shame or condemnation upon us. Romans 8:1 (NIV) says, **"Therefore, there is now no condemnation for those who are in Christ Jesus."** This means that when we fail, God doesn't tear us down; He lifts us so we can grow and become more like Him.

Be Careful What You Watch and Listen To

> *"Life consists of what a man is thinking of all day."* **Ralph Waldo Emerson, American writer and Philosopher.**

When we fill our minds with God's Word, it brings strength to our whole being, spirit, soul, and body. Let's take to heart the wisdom of a father's instructions in the Book of Proverbs, meant to guard our minds and hearts.

Proverbs 4:20–23 (NLT): **"My child, pay attention to what I say; Listen carefully to my words. Don't lose sight of them. Let them penetrate deep into your heart, for they bring life to those who find them, and healing to their whole body."** It feels like a father speaking with urgency and fierce protection: "Never forget these words. Don't let them slip from your sight. Hold them close to your heart like a treasured gift."

This is more than remembering a lesson; it's embracing wisdom until it becomes part of your very identity. The father longs for his son to absorb these truths until they shape his thoughts, guide his decisions, and anchor his actions. Whenever your body feels weak or sick, declare the healing scriptures aloud, repeatedly. Keep speaking even when you don't feel strong enough to do it in the middle of the struggle. Fear and doubt will try to silence you, trying to stop your voice. I urge you to resist that spirit of fear and doubt and keep declaring God's Word with boldness. Faith grows through hearing, and hearing comes through the Word of God.

As I revealed in Chapter 1, when I sank to the lowest point of my life, sick and confined to my bed, all I could hear was the relentless whisper of the enemy: "You will die, there is no hope of healing. Your children will be without a mother." It became a tug-of-war between life and death. I had to push myself to declare healing scriptures again and again, brushing away the heavy dirt of fear and unbelief. Slowly but steadily, my strength returned, and my health was restored.

Your Words Show What's in Your Heart

Jesus taught that our words come from what's inside our hearts. In Matthew 12:34b (NIV), He said, **"For the mouth speaks what the heart is full of."** Just like a tree reveals its fruit, your words reveal the condition of your heart. If your heart is full of joy and love, your words will reflect that. But if it's filled with fear, anxiety, or anger, that will come out too.

Jesus also warned that we will give an account for every careless word we speak. This shows how powerful our words are; they can either build up or tear down. Matthew 12:37 (NIV) says, **"For by your words you will be acquitted, and by your words you will be condemned."**

Proverbs 23:7 says, **"As a man thinks in his heart, so is he."** Your thoughts shape your words and your life. If you keep thinking, "I'm getting weaker," you'll begin to feel weak. If you think, "I'll never be good enough," you'll start living that way. But if you believe, "God has a plan for me," your words and actions will follow that truth.

Look at the life of Job in the Bible. Everything was going well for him, but he feared something bad would happen to his children, and it did. Job 3:25 (NIV): **"What I feared has come upon me; what I dreaded has happened to me."** Later, Job chose to trust God, and the Lord restored everything. Job 42:10 (NIV) says, **"After Job had prayed for his friends, the Lord restored his fortunes and gave him twice as much as he had before."**

Your Words Reveal What You Believe
In Numbers 13, Moses sent twelve men, one leader from each tribe, to explore the land God had promised. Ten of the men returned full of fear, saying, **"We went into the**

land to which you sent us, and it does flow with milk and honey. But the people who live there are powerful, the cities are large and well-fortified, and we even saw descendants of Anak there. We can't attack those people; they are stronger than we are. All the people we saw were giants. We seemed like grasshoppers in our own eyes, and we looked the same to them." These ten men saw themselves as grasshoppers compared to the people of Canaan. They imagined the worst and spread fear to all the Israelites, who also began to see themselves as weak and powerless before the Anakites.

But two, Joshua and Caleb, chose to believe in God's promises. They knew God would help them win. Joshua said**, "Only do not rebel against the Lord. Do not be afraid of the people of the land, because we will swallow them up. Their protection is gone, but the Lord is with us. Do not be afraid of them"** Numbers 14:9 (NIV).

They all saw the same land and the same people, but their thoughts shaped their words, and their words shaped their future. The ten who spoke from the place of fear never entered the promised land, but Joshua and Caleb did.

Speak Faith, Not Fear

Romans 12:2 (NIV) says, **"Do not conform to the pattern of this world, but be transformed by the renewing of your mind..."** So how do we renew our minds? Philippians 4:8 (NIV) guides us to think about things that are true, noble, right, pure, lovely, and admirable.

When you fill your mind with God's truth, your words will begin to align with His will, and your life will overflow with peace and purpose.

God has a beautiful plan for your life. It starts with what you think and what you say. Don't speak words of fear. Don't repeat the lies of the enemy. **Speak faith. Speak the truth. Speak life.** Let your words be rooted in God's promises. Let your heart be filled with His love, so the words from your mouth bring peace, joy, and healing to those around you.

Reflection Questions:

1. What kinds of thoughts usually fill your mind throughout the day — positive, negative, fearful, or hopeful?

2. How do your repeated thoughts (the ones that come up again and again) influence your emotions and decisions?

3. When you notice negative thoughts, how do you typically respond — do you challenge them, or do you let them shape your attitude and words?

4. What would it look like for you to "renew your mind" as Romans 12:2 encourages?

5. Think of a time when your thoughts led you to speak words that caused harm or fear. What could you have done differently?

Closing Prayer:

Heavenly Father,

Thank You for the truth revealed in this chapter, that our words begin with our thoughts, and our thoughts are shaped by what we allow into our minds.

Lord, help us to guard our hearts and renew our minds daily with Your Word. Teach us to recognize Your voice above all others, not the lies of the enemy, not even our own insecurities, but Your voice that speaks life, peace, and purpose.

When fear tries to take over, remind us of Your promises. When negative thoughts rise, help us replace them with truth. Let our hearts be filled with faith so that our words bring encouragement, healing, and hope to those around us.

We choose to plant seeds of truth, to speak life and not fear, and to believe what You say about us. Let our thoughts honor You and let our words reflect Your heart.

In Jesus' name we pray, amen.

CHAPTER 3

Speaking in Power and Authority

Are you just pouring out your problems to God, or are you taking charge and telling those problems to get lost with unwavering faith?

In 2011, my family and I traveled to Austin to celebrate Thanksgiving. I was filled with joy and excitement, looking forward to spending quality time with the people I loved most. We boarded the plane and soon arrived at my brother's house, happy to be together. But I had no idea that within just 15 minutes, everything would take an unexpected turn.

We were enjoying a peaceful evening, sipping tea, and chatting. I got up with my cup of tea in hand, but as I tried to keep it from spilling, I suddenly slipped and fell hard to the floor. I landed on my left hand, and pain shot through my wrist. As I sat there, shocked and hurting, I wondered,

What just happened? Did I do something wrong to deserve this? A wave of self-condemnation came over me.

Then I remembered a scripture I had been meditating on a few weeks earlier:

> **"Every good and perfect gift is from above, and coming down from the Father of heavenly lights, who does not change like shifting shadows" (James 1:17 NIV).**

That verse lit up in my heart. I realized right away that this injury was not a good gift from my loving Heavenly Father. God gives good and perfect things, and this accident didn't come from Him. The enemy was behind it, trying to steal my joy and peace. My perspective changed.

I chose to stand strong and fight the good fight of faith. Since my wrist was swollen and painful, I was sure it was broken. I started declaring healing over it. However, I was rushed to the emergency room. The X-rays confirmed my suspicion; there were multiple fractures. Surgery was needed. They placed a soft cast on my left wrist, and two days later, we returned home.

Back home, I visited an orthopedic surgeon who confirmed the need for surgery, but it would have to wait for six weeks. I had seen God heal me in amazing ways before, but this time, it was hard to hold on to my faith. Many people around me told me surgery was the only answer.

Their words began to affect me. Doubt started creeping in, and unbelief followed. I realized I needed to protect my mind, so I cut off conversations with those who were speaking negatively. I focused on the Word of God. I began rebuking the fear and doubt trying to take over my thoughts and kept declaring, **"By His stripes, I am healed."**

Then, the day before my surgery, I heard a powerful testimony about a baby girl born with a serious heart condition. She was supposed to have a complex surgery, but through prayer, God completely healed her. That story lit a fire in my spirit. I prayed and said, "Lord, if You can give that baby girl a brand new heart, You can surely heal the bones in my wrist." With boldness rising in my heart, I picked up the phone and called the hospital. I canceled my surgery.

What is that big obstacle in your life holding you back from moving forward? Is it fear? Is it pain from the past? Is it doubt, worry, or even a person who keeps pulling you away from God's plan? Don't just talk about it; declare God's powerful words with authority to that obstacle, speak with confidence to the devil and his forces, ordering them to step aside.

Mark 11:22-24 (NIV) tells us, **"Have faith in God, Jesus answered. Truly I tell you, if anyone says to this mountain, go throw yourself into the sea, and do not doubt in their heart but believe that what they say will happen, it will be done for them. Therefore, I tell you, whatever you ask for in prayer, believe that you have received it, and it will be yours."**

There is a difference between speaking to your mountain and speaking about your mountain. Speaking about your mountain will magnify the problems in your mind. The more you talk about it, the bigger and bigger the problems become. However, speaking to your mountain in authority will make it smaller and insignificant.

Jesus made it clear in Mark 11:23 that we should not doubt but believe and then speak. That means you believe once in your heart, but you speak it out more than once. Keep speaking God's truth. Keep declaring victory. Speak healing, peace, strength, and breakthrough. Don't stop until the mountain is gone. One week later, I went back to the doctor for a follow-up and new X-rays. That week felt like the longest, most dreadful week of my life. Every day was a mental battle. Fear tried to take over: What if the healing didn't happen? What if it got worse? What if I die from complications?" I refused to speak those fears aloud. I kept rebuking the enemy and speaking God's promises, **"By His stripes, I am healed."**

Finally, the doctor walked in with the results. My heart began pounding, like a drum beating loudly. I kept quietly repeating to myself that I would not hear a bad report, only a good one. He looked at me with surprise and said, "I don't know what happened, but right now, you don't need surgery. Your bones have somehow shifted back into place, and they're healing just fine."

Praise the Lord! God healed me without surgery!
This experience taught me something I will never forget: the power of speaking to our mountains with faith, not

doubt. When we use the authority God has given us through Jesus Christ, miracles happen. Your words have incredible power. Speak life. Speak faith. Speak healing. God is faithful, and He still performs miracles today!

Your Salvation

Your salvation begins with a right confession of faith in Jesus Christ. When you invite Jesus into your life as Lord and Savior, you are born again. You receive a brand-new spiritual life.

Romans 10:8-9 (NIV) says, **"The word is near you; it is in your mouth and in your heart... If you declare with your mouth, 'Jesus is Lord,' and believe in your heart that God raised Him from the dead, you will be saved."**

When you confess Jesus with your mouth, your new life begins.

2 Corinthians 5:17 (NIV) reminds us, **"Therefore, if anyone is in Christ, he is a new creation; old things have passed away; behold, all things have become new."**

Let's explore this new life in three parts: Spirit, Soul, and Body.

Spirit

When you are born again, your spirit becomes brand new, completely holy, and perfect. Why? Because Jesus, the hope of glory, now lives in you. Colossians 1:27b (NIV) says, **"...Christ in you, the hope of glory."** Since His Spirit now lives in you, you can manifest the fruit of the Spirit: Love, joy, peace, patience, kindness, goodness, faithfulness, gentleness, and self-control.

Soul

Your soul includes your mind, will, emotions, and memories. Even after salvation, your soul still needs healing. You may remember past wounds, childhood trauma, shame, guilt, or unforgiveness. These don't disappear overnight. That's why the Bible tells us to renew our minds through meditating on Scripture.

Galatians 5:19-21 (NIV) warns us about the works of the flesh, such as sexual immorality, impurity, jealousy, anger, strife, hatred, and more. These come from the soul and the flesh and must be overcome through renewing your mind with God's Word.

You need soul healing, freedom from bitterness, release from shame, and restoration in broken places. The journey takes time, but God is faithful to renew and transform you.

Body

Your physical body is essential too. Scripture says your body is the Temple of the Holy Spirit. 1 Corinthians 6:19 (NIV) says, ***Do you not know that your bodies are the temple of the Holy Spirit, who is in you, whom you have received from God? You are not your own.*** Because your body belongs to God, you are called to honor Him with it. Romans 12:1 (NIV) says, ***Therefore, I urge you, brothers and sisters, in view of God's mercy, to offer your bodies as*** *a living sacrifice, holy and pleasing to God, this is your true and proper worship."*

Know Your Identity in Christ

Your identity is no longer based on your past, your failures, or what others say about you.

Your true **identity** is found in **Christ!**

Declare who you are in Christ.
Speak these identifiers daily:

I am a child of God. (John 1:12)

I am forgiven. (1 John 1:9)

I am healed. (1 Peter 2:24)

I am chosen. (1 Peter 2:9)

I am free. (John 8:36)

I am deeply loved. (Romans 5:8)

I am filled with the Spirit of God. (Romans 8:9)

I am Christ's friend. (John 15:15)

I am united with the Lord. (1 Corinthians 6:17)

I am complete in Christ. (Colossians 2:10)

I am free forever from condemnation. (Romans 8:1-2)

I am assured all things work for good. (Romans 8:28)

I am free from any charge against me. (Romans 8:33)

I am established, anointed, and sealed by God. (2 Corinthians 1:21-22)

I am hidden with Christ in God. (Colossians 3:3)

I'm a citizen of Heaven. I am significant. (Philippines 3:20-21)

I am the salt of the earth. (Matthew 5:13)

I am the light of the world. (Mathew 5:14)

I am the branch of the true vine, a channel of His life. (John 15:1-5)

I am a personal witness of Christ. (Acts 1:8)

I am God's Temple. (1 Corinthians 3:16)

I am a minister of reconciliation. (2 Corinthians 5:17-19)

I am the ambassador of Christ. (2 Corinthians 5:20)

I am God's co-worker. (1 Corinthians 3:9)

I am seated with Christ in heavenly realms. (Ephesians 2:6)

I am God's workmanship. (Ephesians 2:10)

Live boldly in your true identity, redeemed, restored, and empowered in Christ Jesus!

As you continue speaking these truths over yourself, you will begin to develop the mind of Christ. There will be times in life when you feel worthless, unloved, or completely defeated. In those moments, it's easy to believe you're a failure and question the very reason for living. I remember going through days like that, dark, lonely days when I believed every lie the enemy whispered. I thought I'd never break free from the weight of those painful emotions.

But everything shifted when I received a fresh revelation from God's Word, specifically in Revelation Chapter 1. I discovered that God has already called us kings and priests through Christ Jesus.

Revelation 1:5b-6 (NKJV) says: **"To Him who loved us and washed us from our sins in His own blood, and has made us kings and priests to His God and Father, to Him be glory and dominion forever and ever. Amen."** This truth changed everything. I realized that if God has called me as a king and a priest, then I am not weak or worthless. I am anointed like a priest, and I carry the authority of a king. As Ecclesiastes 8:4 (NKJV) declares: **"Where the word of a king is, there is power; and who may say to him, 'What are you doing?"** A king's word carries power. No one dares to challenge the decisions or declarations of a king. And because you are in Christ, you walk in that same spiritual authority. Job 22:28 (NKJV) confirms this: **"You will also decree a thing, and it will be established for you; so light will shine on your ways."** When you speak in faith, grounded in God's Word, heaven moves. Your declarations bring breakthroughs. Your words, filled with the truth of God's promises, carry the power to change your life.

A Personal Story

In 2005, I experienced chest pain and high blood pressure, so I was taken to the hospital. After running some tests, the doctor prescribed medicine for high blood pressure, but it caused my pressure to drop too low. Because of that, they stopped the medication and sent me home. The final diagnosis was a pulled muscle; my heart was fine.

A week later, I saw my primary doctor. He asked if I was still taking the medicine prescribed. I explained I was told to discontinue it because my pressure had dropped too low. He looked surprised and said, "You should never stop taking your medicine. Don't you know you're a heart patient?" I was never diagnosed as a heart patient at the hospital. In fact, my pain on that visit was due to muscle strain. I was confused by the primary physician's bold statement that I was a heart patient. Those words shook me. Was I really a heart patient? Or was fear trying to get a grip on me? What you feel and think from your emotions can become the wrong language.

I spoke aloud, "No! I cancel those word curses in Jesus' name. I am not a heart patient." I refused to let those words take root in my heart. Instead, I declared, "By His stripes I am healed. My heart is strong and healthy." I chose to believe what God says in His Word. Today, by His grace, I am healthy. That's the power of speaking God's truth over fear. It's time for us to rise and speak into existence the things we want to see in our lives. When you declare something in faith, God will establish it. That is His promise.

So, what's been holding you back?

I know it's not easy when you're dealing with pain, pressure, or heartache at the moment. Forgiving can feel impossible. Letting go is hard when your heart is wounded. But Jesus doesn't want you stuck in that dark, difficult place. He loves you more than you realize and has a powerful purpose for your life. Right now, He's calling you to rise and come out of the pit.

Think about Joseph in the book of Genesis. His brothers threw him into a pit and sold him as a slave. Life only got harder. He was falsely accused, imprisoned, forgotten, and alone. But Joseph didn't let the pain define him. He never gave up on the dreams God had placed in his heart. He kept trusting, and in time, God lifted him. Joseph went from the pit to the palace and became second in command over all of Egypt.

Don't lose sight of what Jesus did for you on the Cross. He declared, "It is finished." That means the work is complete. He conquered sin, sickness, and every force of the enemy for the last time. Now He's calling you to walk in the authority He has given you.

In Luke 10:19 (NIV), Jesus says, **"I have given you the authority to trample on serpents and scorpions and over all the power of the enemy, and nothing shall harm you."** You are anointed. You carry spiritual authority.

Speak God's Word with boldness. Don't just talk about your problems, declare what you want to see happen. Speak life, healing, peace, and restoration. Call things that are not as though they already are. That's the language of faith. Embrace your identity as a king and priest in Christ. Let your words bring transformation to your life and those around you. You carry power through Jesus; use it.

Reflection Questions:

1. What mountain are you facing right now?

2. Are you speaking about it or speaking to it?

3. What words are you declaring daily?

4. Do you honestly believe God's Word over your emotions?

5. Are there negative voices in your life that you need to turn down so you can hear God's voice more clearly?

Closing Prayer:

Lord Jesus, thank You for giving me authority through Your name. Help me to speak in faith, not fear. Let Your Word be the first thing on my lips every day. Teach me to declare truth, resist the enemy, and walk in victory. Amen.

CHAPTER 4

Watch Your Words

Have you ever found yourself saying something in the heat of the moment, only to realize it caused pain? In this chapter, let's take a closer look at our emotions and their influence on how we speak. Pausing to think before speaking is like extending a caring hand to those we interact with. Being mindful of our words is a tangible way to express care and consideration, emphasizing the importance of choosing language that leaves a positive imprint on both us and those around us.

It all started with a seemingly innocent water fountain my husband put in the middle of the driveway. Oddly enough, it became a symbol of my growing frustration. Every time I backed up my car, anxiety and irritation took over, fearing I might accidentally damage the fountain. The clash between my wish for a clear driveway and my husband's love for this decorative piece resulted in a few flat tires. I kept expressing my dislike for the fountain, and this simmering anger stuck around for about two to three years.

One day, as I was singing and praising God, I approached my car. As I began to reverse, I felt an all-too-familiar wave of rage welling up inside me. But this time, something was different. I hit the brakes. I realized that the anger I harbored towards my husband was not just about a mere water fountain. It was a manifestation of something deeper, something the enemy had exploited to hold me captive in a stronghold of anger. It was as if the same mouth I used to praise God became a weapon, having an inner dialogue of negative words towards my husband.

There's an old Arab proverb that says, *"The tongue is the messenger of the heart."* This means that our spoken words reflect what's in our hearts. The way we speak can reveal our true feelings and intentions.

That moment marked the beginning of deeper healing. I began to pray, reflect, and invite God into those hidden places of frustration. It reminded me how easily the enemy can twist our emotions when we're not anchored in truth.

How can you bless and curse with the same mouth? This should not be. James 3:9-10 (NIV) says, **"With the tongue we praise our Lord and Father, and with it we curse human beings, who have been made in God's likeness. Out of the same mouth comes praise and cursing. My brothers and sisters, this should not be."** That day marked the end of my angry episodes about the water fountain. It was a silent victory, known only to me.

Jesus emphasized the importance of our words. In Matthew 12:34b-35 (NKJV), He said, **"...For out of the abundance of the heart the mouth speaks. A good man out of the good treasure of his heart brings forth good things, and an evil man out of the evil treasure brings forth evil things."**

Imagine your words as messengers of your inner self. If kindness, joy, and love reside in your heart, your words likely carry warmth, peace, and encouragement. This positive energy becomes a magnet, drawing people toward you. Conversely, if you struggle with anger, unforgiveness, or resentment, your words might bear the weight of hurt, judgment, or condemnation. Unfortunately, this negativity repels others, making it challenging to connect with people.

Let us look into Matthew 5:22 (NASB): **"But I say to you that whoever is angry with his brother shall be guilty before the court; and whoever says to his brother, 'You good for nothing,' shall be guilty before the supreme court; and whoever says, 'You fool,' shall be guilty enough to go into the fiery hell."** Jesus is serious about the way we use our words.

To follow Jesus's example, we should use wholesome words and avoid speaking carelessly. As mentioned in Colossians 4:6, our conversations should be filled with grace and wisdom, so that we respond to everyone respectfully. Jesus also warned us about the consequences of our words in Matthew 12:36-37. He said that we will be held accountable for every idle word we speak. *Our words can either justify us or condemn us.* The words we speak will either work for or against us. Jesus said we will be justified or condemned by the words of our mouths. He is not condemning us to go to hell. He's talking about the things we can have in this life by **speaking.**

William Arthur Ward, an American motivational writer, quoted **"*A complaining tongue reveals an ungrateful heart*."**

An ungrateful attitude is something most of us are unaware that we have, but everyone else sees it. An ungrateful person will complain or murmur about almost anything.

Numbers 11 tells us the story of how God's people complained and murmured against God. God gave them manna, but the people were not satisfied with that. God was providing what His people needed in the desert, but they wanted more; they wanted meat. The constant complaining angered God. To become angry, frustrated, and dissatisfied with what we have may be the greatest temptation we face today.

1 Corinthians 10:10-11(NLT) says, **"And don't grumble as some of them did and then were destroyed by the angel of death. These things happened to them as examples for us. They were written down to warn us who live at the end of the age."** God wants us to be careful with our words.

Apostle Paul admonishes us in Philippians 2:14 (NLT), **"Do everything without complaining and arguing, so that no one can criticize you. Live clean, innocent lives as children of God, shining like bright lights in a world full of crooked and perverse people."**

Ephesians 4:29 (NIV) admonishes, **"Do not let any unwholesome talk come out of your mouths, but only what is helpful for building others up according to their needs, that it may benefit those who listen."**

People could feel Jesus' love, even when His Words were challenging. He balanced grace and truth. The Bible says, **"In the beginning was the Word, and the Word was with God, and the Word was God." It also tells us, "And the Word became flesh and lived among us. We saw his glory, the glory of the one and only Son, full of grace and truth"** (John 1:1, 14 NIV). This shows the deep connection between Jesus, who is described as the Word, and the qualities of grace and truth.

When we're upset or angry, our words can hurt others. In my own experience, my Aunt Mary and her hurtful words wounded me profoundly. It led to struggles with insecurity, low self-esteem, and feeling unworthy. I thought and spoke negatively from that place of pain. It's like hurting people ending up hurting others. At that time, I didn't realize I was doing it. But once I forgave my aunt and others, my healing began, and I tried to become a source of joy for those around me.

Jesus said in Matthew 6:14-15 (NIV), **"For if you forgive other people when they sin against you, your Heavenly Father will also forgive you. But if you do not forgive others their sins, your father will not forgive your sins."**

When I forgave my aunt and let go of all judgment, it was like a comforting blanket of peace wrapped around me, a peace beyond words. Talking about her no longer brought emotional pain. Now, I view my aunt with a more compassionate perspective, even though I wish she had accepted Christ before she passed away.

Fear and insecurity associated with anxiety can lead to defensive outbursts of anger when individuals feel threatened. I've been through this myself, especially when my husband rushes me to keep up with his fast pace, while I'm naturally more slow-paced. In those moments, I find myself getting defensive and angry, saying things I don't mean. It's a challenge, but disciplining myself to speak the truth from God's Word has been crucial in these situations.

I would recite Psalm 19:14 (NKJV) **"Let the words of my mouth and meditation of my heart be acceptable in Your sight, O Lord, my strength and my Redeemer."** The Psalmist is praying for complete integrity that our inner thoughts and our outward words would align and both be holy before God. It's a nudge to choose our words wisely and to speak in a positive, thoughtful way.

Carl Jung, a psychoanalyst, wrote, *"Everything that irritates us about others can lead us to an understanding of ourselves."*

When we bury negative emotions and speak harshly about ourselves or others, we ultimately wound our own hearts. It's essential to acknowledge our feelings and stay mindful of the words we choose to receive or speak. After Elijah struck down the prophets of Baal, he was terrified by Jezebel's death threat and fled into the wilderness, where he sank into deep despair and begged God to let him die. (1 Kings 19:4-14, NIV) Even though Elijah was bold enough to defeat 450 false prophets, he became paralyzed by Jezebel's deadly decree against him.

Healing from Hidden Sin

I used to secretly attend a church group that my husband forbade me from participating in. I lied about where I was because I irrationally feared he would kill me if he found out. I felt justified since it was a Bible study, but deep down I knew it was wrong. One day, a preacher spoke about truth, saying, "Lying is easy, but speaking the truth may cost you your life. Peter denied Jesus three times; otherwise, it would have cost him his life." His message convicted me, and I decided I would stop lying, no matter the consequences.

The next time I went to the Bible study, I told my husband the truth. To my surprise, nothing terrible happened. The fear I lived in was louder than the reality. I learned this: Don't lie to escape consequences. It steals your peace and joy. Truth brings freedom.

Ephesians 4:26-27 (NIV) says, **"'In your anger do not sin': Do not let the sun go down while you are still angry, and do not give the devil a foothold."**

Ever felt like **unforgiveness** opens a door for negativity to creep into your heart? According to James 1:19-20, **it's a good call to be quick to listen, slow to speak, and slow to anger. Because, you see, human anger doesn't lead to the righteousness of God**. Holding on to grudges is like giving the enemy a foothold in your soul. But forgiveness? That's your key to shutting that door and reconciling with those who've wronged you.

"Never say mean words out of anger. Your anger will pass, but your words will scar a person for life." - Author Stephanie J. Brown.

Matthew 7:1-2 (NIV) says, **"Do not judge or you will be judged. For in the same way you judge others, you will be judged, and with the measure you use, it will be measured to you."** Judging others gives the demonic realm a legal right to torment you. The more we judge others, the more we will be tormented. See the beautiful quote from Saint Mother Teresa, a Catholic nun and the founder of the Missionaries of Charity in Calcutta, India. *"If you judge people, you have no time to love them."*

A Secret Vow:

The solemn promise I made to myself during my teenage years has left a lasting negative impact on my children. This kind of vow can be an unhealthy commitment we create in an attempt to ensure our security or protect ourselves and others in the face of traumatic experiences. Such inner vows often stem from the scars of trauma or the dysfunction within families or experiences of abuse.

Imagine a young teenage girl making a silent pledge to herself during a deeply troubling ordeal.

Proverbs 20:25 (NIV) warns, **"It is a trap to dedicate something rashly and only later to consider one's vows."**

When we make an inner vow, we turn to ourselves rather than to God.

During my time living with my Aunt Mary, her controlling behavior made me feel like I was enslaved, depriving me of a normal childhood. Consequently, I harbored an intense fear that my children might suffer a similar fate if I ever allowed them to venture anywhere without my constant supervision. Driven by this fear, I became overly protective of them, constantly worrying about their well-being and striving to shield them from the hardships I endured.

I can still recall my children's pleas, as they grew older, asserting their independence and expressing their desire not to be treated like toddlers. I attended a Sozo Ministry session, which led me into the depths of my own childhood trauma. I uncovered something deeply rooted and unexpected: an inner vow I had made as a little girl. I had promised myself I would never leave my children with anyone, not even for a moment. That vow was made long before they were born. With a heart open to healing, I repented and chose to break that vow, releasing both myself and my children from its quiet grip.

Our gracious God is known for his boundless love and endless mercy. First John 1:9 reminds us that when we confess our sins, He's faithful and just to forgive us and to cleanse us from all unrighteousness. When we sin, we often feel weighed down by our mistakes, with feelings of guilt, shame, and condemnation. We feel as if they are in our memories forever. However, our Almighty God is different. When we truly repent and seek His forgiveness, He not only pardons us but forgets our sins altogether.

My aunt used to say repeatedly that God would punish me for my wrongdoings. Her words echoed in my ears throughout my life. I lived in a constant state of guilt, self-condemnation, self-pity, and unworthiness. I grew up feeling like I could never truly please God, and that He was always watching me with judgment, ready to punish me for every mistake.

One day, I took my son to a youth Bible study. The youth pastor taught from Romans 8:1 (NIV), **"Therefore, there is now no condemnation for those who are in Christ Jesus."** He explained that God is not looking to punish us. Instead, He loves us unconditionally. The pastor said that conviction comes from God, but condemnation does not. It comes from the enemy. That moment was a huge revelation for me. A wave of freedom washed over me, breaking the spirit of guilt, self-pity, and self-condemnation that had held me down for so long.

Let us consider the scriptures that highlight God not remembering our sins once He forgives us.

Hebrews 8:12 (NIV): **"For I will forgive their wickedness and will remember their sins no more."** This verse means that God will forgive and will not remember people's wrongdoings or sins.

Isaiah 43:25 (NKJV): **"I, even I, am He that blot out your transgressions for Mine own sake, and will not remember your sins."** We may remember our or others' past sins, but God will not.

Hebrews 10:17 (NIV): **"and their sins and their lawless acts I will remember no more."**

Isaiah 44:22 (NIV): **"I have bloated out, like a thick cloud, your transgressions, and like a cloud, your sins. Return to Me, for I have redeemed you."**

Imagine you're painting a wall that has tough stains and marks. When you're done, those stubborn spots are nowhere to be seen. That's what Jesus does for you. His precious blood cleanses you, making you as pure as snow. Your sins are forgiven, and in His eyes, you're righteous and flawless.

> **Micah 7:19 (NKJV): "He will again have compassion on us, and will subdue our iniquities. You will cast our sins into the depths of the sea."**

Think of it like tossing a stone into a vast ocean; it sinks deep, way down. Our loving God does something similar with our sins. He washes them away, burying them deep in the ocean of forgiveness. That leaves us feeling relieved and ready for a fresh start. Our words reflect our hearts, and Jesus teaches us to use them wisely and positively. We have seen how anger, frustration, and ungratefulness can lead to hurtful words and negative consequences.

We are reminded of the incredible love and forgiveness of God, who not only forgives our sins but also forgets them entirely. We should strive to be more like Jesus in our words and actions, spreading love, kindness, and understanding in our interactions with others. By doing so, we can create a more positive and harmonious world for ourselves and those around us.

Reflection Questions:

1. Have you ever said something out of anger that you later regretted? What happened, and how did it make you feel afterward?

2. What do you think it means to "watch your words"? Why is it important?

3. Which Bible verse from this chapter spoke to your heart the most? Why do you think it stood out to you?

4. Are there any "inner vows" or promises you've made to yourself out of fear or pain? How might God want to help you let go of those?

5. Can you think of someone you've judged or spoken harshly to? What steps can you take to show them love and forgiveness?

6. When was the last time your words helped someone else feel encouraged or loved? How did that make you feel?

Closing Prayer:

Dear Heavenly Father,

Thank You for the gift of words and the power they carry. I confess that sometimes I speak from hurt, fear, or anger rather than from love and truth. Please forgive me for every careless word I've spoken and help me to speak life, not death, to myself and others.

Lord, I surrender any inner vows or wounds that have shaped the way I communicate. Heal my heart and renew my mind. Teach me to speak with grace, wisdom, and compassion, as Jesus did.

Thank You for Your mercy that not only forgives but forgets. Help me to forgive others as You've forgiven me and to walk in freedom from the past. May my words reflect Your love and bring peace to those around me.

In Jesus' name,
Amen.

Faith Speaks

Within the pages of Chapter 5, we embark on a trans-formative journey where faith becomes a vocal force, speaking truth into the depths of our existence. "Faith Speaks" is not just a chapter title; it's an invitation to witness the dynamic interplay between belief and spoken words. Join me as we unravel the mysteries of faith and explore the incredible power of declarations.

What is faith?

> Now faith is the substance of things hoped for, and evidence of things not seen. Hebrews 11:1(NKJV)

It is the reality of what we hope for, and it is the evidence of things we cannot see yet.

Life is full of challenges, and it is easy to get discouraged when things don't go as planned. Instead of dwelling on the negatives, faith encourages you to focus on the possibilities. It speaks to your inner self, telling you that setbacks are temporary and that brighter days are ahead.

I made a faith confession back in 2014. I was having challenges completing a master's in Christian counseling. The anxiety was overwhelming, and doubts about my ability to finish the course were overtaking me. I knew God was calling me to do this. However, I was going to give up. I felt like I was a failure. I cried out to God for help. Then, unexpectedly, a ray of hope pierced through.

One day, out of nowhere, I began picturing myself confidently walking across the stage on graduation day. Gratitude welled up within me as I thanked God for that impending, glorious moment. In my mind's eye, I saw myself in my cap and gown, ascending the stage, and proudly accepting my degree. Fueled by faith, I began to declare, **".. with God all things are possible."** Matthew 19:26b (NIV). This is far more than the power of positive thinking. It is the power of God that makes what seems impossible possible. **Nothing is impossible for God.** Luke 1:37 (CEV).

With unwavering conviction, I proclaimed loudly and boldly that I would indeed graduate in May 2015. My mantra became, "I can do all things through Christ Jesus who strengthens me" (Philippians 4:13). It was a declaration that echoed not only with determination but with a deep sense of dependence on a power greater than me.

Faith is the language of the soul. It is not silent; it speaks clearly and boldly. Faith confidently speaks the words that God has said. It does not speak only once. It speaks repeatedly and consistently about what God has said. We can see in 2 Corinthians 4:13 (NKJV) "And since we have the same spirit of faith, according to what is written, 'I **believed** therefore I **spoke**,' We also believe, therefore, **speak**."

Faith is made of two main components: **believing in the heart** and **speaking with the mouth.** We know that God has given every man the measure of faith (Romans 12:13). What you really believe will be spoken out of your mouth. We can see in Romans 10:17 that faith comes by hearing and hearing by the Word of God.

How Can Faith Work in Your Life?

Faith comes by hearing, and it is released by speaking. We must both believe and speak our faith for it to do the work.

I went through a tough time battling fear and doubt, worried that I wouldn't graduate in 2015. I began speaking God's word and picturing myself confidently walking across the stage on graduation day. That gave me the motivation and discipline to consistently and persistently tackle my coursework. As my graduation day neared, I pushed myself to complete my courses in time. My faith confession worked!

On May 16, 2015, I graduated. It turned out to be one of the happiest days of my life. I took God at His Word and aligned my words with His. When I direct my faith in the right direction through spoken declarations, I experience the goodness of God. It's amazing how believing and speaking positively can bring about such incredible outcomes.

The principle of believing and speaking is also shown in Romans 10:8-10 (NASB). How did you get saved? "But what does it say? 'The word is near you, in your mouth and in your heart' (that is, the word of faith we preach): that if you confess with your mouth Jesus as Lord, and believe in your heart that God raised him from the dead, you will be saved; for with the heart a person believes, resulting in righteousness, and with the mouth he confesses, resulting in salvation." Our **salvation** is based on **believing** and **speaking**.

Speak to Your Mountains

Mark 11:23 (NKJV) says, **"For assuredly, I say to you, whoever says to this mountain, 'Be removed and be cast into the sea,' and does not doubt in his heart, but believes that those things he says will be done, he will have whatever he says."**

In the journey of life, we often face challenges that seem as daunting as mountains. The mountains we face may be physical, spiritual, emotional, mental, financial, or marital (to mention a few). It's during these times that a powerful lesson from Mark 11:23 can inspire and guide us. It tells us a simple yet profound truth about the power of faith and words. Imagine having the ability to speak to a literal mountain and commanding it to move into the sea!

We can learn three important things from this verse.

1. Faith without Doubt

The scripture emphasizes the importance of having faith without a hint of doubt in our hearts. Doubt can act as an obstacle, hindering the manifestation of our desires. To speak with faith means to express our hopes and beliefs without reservation, trusting that what we say will indeed come to pass.

2. Believing in Spoken Words

The key lies in genuinely believing that the things we speak will be accomplished. It's not merely uttering words; it's about cultivating a deep-seated belief that our spoken affirmations have the power to shape our reality. This requires a profound sense of trust in the unseen forces at work in our lives.

3. Having Whatever We Say

The promise embedded in this verse is powerful: "He will have whatever he says." This isn't a magical word but a testament to the connection between faith, words, and manifestation. Our spoken words, rooted in unwavering faith, can bring about the changes we desire, just like the mountain being cast into the sea.

How to Apply 'Faith Speaking' in Our Lives: Personal Testimony

Flashback to 1983, right after graduating from nursing college. I landed a night shift job in the nursery as a registered nurse, responsible for forty newborns alongside two other nurses. Our task: observe and feed babies every three to four hours. In those days, we prepared formulas and washed bottles ourselves. As a new nurse, I was anxious, fearing potential medical issues for the babies. Night after night, I walked in fear, vigilant to ensure no newborn faced troubles.

After a month of stressful night shifts, chest pain, and palpitations landed me in the hospital—diagnosis: Mitral Valve Prolapse, a heart condition. The prescription was clear: no more night shifts, a lifetime of medications. I was incredibly sad at the news that, as a young woman, I would need to be on medications for the rest of my life. It did not sit well with me.

Six months post-diagnosis, I attended a small prayer group at someone's home. An evangelist prayed and declared healing in the name of the Lord Jesus. Without a doubt, I received the word. That evening, I stopped my medications. Although chest pain and palpitations persisted with exertion, my faith surpassed the symptoms. [A side note: I will not and do not advocate for anyone stopping their medications as I did].

Days became weeks, and weeks turned into a month. With every moment, my trust in God's promise grew stronger. By faith, I kept declaring the healing scriptures over myself. The chest pain and palpitations, once powerful enemies, now felt like distant memories from the past. I had overcome not just a health issue but also the fear and doubt that tried to hold me captive.

Recognize and confront doubt when it arises. Instead of letting it take root, replace it with affirmations of faith. All healings are not instant. Sometimes, it can take weeks or months. Surround yourself with positive influences that reinforce your beliefs and uplift your spirit.

Let us look at Abraham, the Father of Faith. His faith confession serves as an inspiring example for believers of all ages. In Romans 4:19-20, we learn that despite his advanced age and his wife Sarah's infertility, Abraham did not let his faith waver. At nearly 100 years old, he faced the reality of his own body and Sarah's barren womb. Yet, he stood firm in faith, refusing to doubt the promises of God. Instead, he found strength in his belief, giving glory to God. Abraham was fully convinced that God, who had made the promise, was also capable of fulfilling it.

Picture this: Abraham is nearly a centenarian, and Sarah is almost ninety years old. God had promised them descendants as numerous as the stars. Despite the seemingly insurmountable challenges, Abraham's faith confession began with embracing this extraordinary promise. God went on to rename Abram to Abraham and Sarai to Sarah, declaring them parents of nations even before Sarah conceived.

Abraham's journey wasn't without obstacles. He grappled with age and Sarah's infertility. Yet, his faith confession resonated louder than his circumstances. Despite the natural impossibility of conceiving a child, Abraham chose to actively trust God's promise. His faith was not merely passive; it was a vocal declaration of righteousness, credited to him as such in Genesis 15:6. Notably, Sarah gave birth to the promised child at the remarkable age of ninety.

In facing challenges, doubt becomes a weapon wielded by the enemy to hinder belief in God's word. Doubt and unbelief breed fear, activating the adversary. On the contrary, faith activates God. When life's storm rages, maintaining focus on God brings perfect peace, as Isaiah 26:3 attests. **Fear activates the devil. Faith activates God.**

The principle of aligning our words with God's is crucial for a victorious life. Hebrews 10:23 urges believers to hold fast to their hope without wavering, to what God has promised. Keeping our words in agreement with God is essential to receiving His promises.

I fondly recall a dear family member who, out of fear, often spoke unsettling words for years. Whenever she experienced pain in her head or stomach, despite good lab results, she would express anxiety, fearing she might have cancer. When other family members fell ill, she'd dread the possibility of cancer. Sadly, she passed away from cancer. It is a touching reminder that the adversary seeks to steal, kill, and destroy. We must resist the voice of the enemy, preventing his will from taking root in our lives. Remembering Jesus's words in John 10:10b (NIV): **"I have come that they may have life, and they may have it more abundantly,"** we are engaged to embrace a life of abundance. Faith speaks; unfortunately, she spoke from a foundation rooted in fear.

Consider this: during the flu season, speaking fear, such as anticipating illness for yourself and your children, releases doubt and activates negative forces. What we think and speak manifests in our lives. Meditating on circumstances leads to self-fulfilling prophecies. Ultimately, what you imagine determines what you believe, and what you believe determines how you receive it. But if you meditate on what God's Word has to say, you will conceive what God's Word says. It will change everything about you - how you see yourself and your circumstances. That is powerful!

You can say, "By the stripes of Lord Jesus I am healed. I take authority over this virus in the name of Jesus. I plead the blood of Jesus over my family and me in the name of Jesus. None of us will get sick in the flu season."

When you allow faith to speak in your life, you are essentially transforming your thoughts into reality. Your mindset shifts from doubt and unbelief to confidence and hope. Your mouth has so much power and authority that you do not want to use your mouth to confess things that bring actual destruction over yourself or others. We must agree with God and the words of life over our situation.

Faith is not a passive belief; it is an active force that can shape your reality. When faith speaks, it echoes a message of hope, resilience, and the potential for miracles. So let your faith speak loud and clear and watch as it transforms your life in ways you never thought possible.

Be encouraged as you relax in knowing that Father God loves you immensely. He has already made a way out of life's difficult circumstances by sending Jesus to meet all your needs for deliverance, healing, and preservation. Find what He has promised you in the Bible. Have faith in the WORD, **believe** it, and **speak** it. As a result, you can have a confident expectation that God will do what He said. Continually **believe and speak** with gratitude until you see His promise manifested. Remember, **Faith Speaks**!

Reflection Questions:

1. What are you currently believing in God for that seems impossible in the natural world? How can you begin to speak life and truth over that situation?

2. Have your words lined up more with faith or with fear lately? What changes do you feel the Holy Spirit is prompting you to make in your speech?

3. Can you recall a time when your faith confession brought a breakthrough? How did that experience strengthen your walk with God?

4. When fear or doubt creeps in, what scriptures can you begin to declare aloud to strengthen your faith?

5. How has the story of Abraham, or the author's testimony, encouraged you to trust God's promises more fully? In what areas do you need to "call things that are not as though they were"? (Romans 4:17)

6. What "mountains" are you facing today? How can you apply Mark 11:23 in your prayers and declarations?

7. Do you believe your words hold spiritual power? If so, how might that truth impact the way you speak about your health, family, future, and daily life?

Closing Prayer:

Heavenly Father,

Thank You for the gift of faith and the power of the words You have given us. You spoke the world into being, and You've called us to speak with that same Spirit of faith. Lord, help us to believe Your Word deeply and to speak it boldly, especially when challenges arise. Let our mouths be filled with declarations of life, hope, healing, and victory.

Forgive us for the times we've spoken words of doubt, fear, or frustration. Help us to align our words with Your truth. Holy Spirit, remind us daily that faith comes by hearing, and let us hear the Word of God continually until it takes deep root in our hearts.

May we speak to our mountains with authority, just as Jesus taught, and see them move. Let our testimonies bring glory to You and encouragement to others. Strengthen us, Lord, to hold fast to our confession without wavering, for You who promised are faithful.

In Jesus' mighty name,
Amen.

CHAPTER 6

Say 'Yes and Amen'

> "For no matter how many promises God has made, they are 'Yes' in Christ. And so through Him the 'Amen' is spoken by us to the glory of God." - 2 Corinthians 1:20 (NIV)

Every promise God gives is a loud and clear "Yes." His Word is our unshakable guarantee.

A promise is sacred. It's more than words; it's a commitment that should never be broken. We hold on to promises because they help us move forward, stay grounded, and find hope, even in hard times.

The Bible is filled with God's promises, over 7,000 of them! Psalm 119:89 (NIV) says, **"Forever, O Lord, Your Word is settled in heaven."** In a world where everything keeps changing, nothing feels permanent. But God's Word is forever, unchanging, and fully secure. Our God is eternal. He never breaks His promises.

Have you ever waited on a promise, hoping with all your heart, only to feel the sting of disappointment when it didn't come?

Let me take you back. When my mom left my siblings and me with Aunt Mary, she told us she'd be back soon. Every night, I held on to that promise. I imagined her walking through the door with my dad, smiling, hugging us tight. But days became months. Months stretched into years. Do you know what it's like to keep waiting and feel that promise slipping further away with every sunrise?

For eight long years, I hoped and prayed for my parents to return. I missed them every single day. Tears would fall in the quiet of the night. The pain of that empty promise weighed heavily on my heart. And when I became a teenager, everything inside me felt like it was falling apart. Emotionally and physically, I was a mess. I needed my mom more than ever during those years when you're changing, growing, unsure, and want someone to say, "I'm here." You need a steady voice in the storm. Being a teenager is tough and not having your mom there is even harder.

As I was heading off to college, my mom finally came back. The promise was technically fulfilled. But it felt like it came too late. Those years without her had already left their mark. I was still carrying the weight of waiting. The hurt didn't just disappear.

Chief Joseph, a leader of the Nez Perce, an Indian tribe, once said, **"It makes my heart sick when I remember all**

the good words and the broken promises." Have you ever felt that kind of pain?

Promises Are Like Building Blocks of Trust

In marriage, we stand before God and people and make sacred vows to stick together through sickness, financial stress, and whatever else life throws our way. We joyfully say, "I do, I do, I do." I remember a family friend who entered marriage with the same hopeful promises. The husband, trusting his wife's word, asked her to help contribute half of the family's income. She agreed without hesitation. In essence, she said, "Yes and Amen" to the life they promised to build together.

But then reality hit. She didn't keep her word. Their home became filled with arguments and stress, even in front of their children. The husband, hurt and disappointed, kept reminding her of the promise she made. The tension grew worse over time. Eventually, the wife couldn't handle it anymore. After ten long years of struggle, they divorced.

This painful story shows how powerful broken promises can be. A single unkept promise can begin to unravel even the strongest bonds. It reminds us how serious our words are, especially in relationships. **"It is better not to make a promise than to make one and not keep it."** (Ecclesiastes 5:5 GW).

Don't Make Promises You Can't Keep

My family carries the weight of an unfulfilled promise. When our children were little, my husband promised he'd build them a basketball court. They were excited and hopeful. But life had other plans. Unforeseen circumstances came up, and the dream never happened. We didn't mean to let them down. We wanted to keep our word. But sometimes, life throws us curveballs that interrupt even our best intentions. That's when we need grace. Grace for ourselves. Grace for each other. And the understanding that sometimes things don't go as planned.

How Do We Embrace God's Promises?

Second Peter 1:4 says God hasn't just given us promises. He's given us *exceedingly great and precious promises*. Through His Word, He reveals what He's already provided, and those promises give us strength to face whatever comes our way. And here's the beautiful part: God's promises can never be broken.

God is the *ultimate* promise keeper. Let's look again at 2 Corinthians 1:20 (NIV): **"For no matter how many promises God has made, they are 'Yes' in Christ."** That means every single promise God makes is already confirmed! He's saying, "Yes!" Now, it's up to us to say, "Amen!" That's our way of responding, our way of saying, "Let it be true in my life." It's not a one-sided deal. It's a partnership, God speaks, and we agree. He declares the promise, and we respond in kind.

Let's go back to the beginning, to God's first promise. In Genesis 1:28 (NKJV), God blesses humanity and says, **"Be fruitful and multiply; fill the earth and subdue it; have dominion..."** He was giving us a divine purpose: a calling to increase, lead, and care for what He created. That wasn't just for Adam and Eve. That promise is still alive today. God wants us to walk in it.

He's cheering us on to grow, lead, and be caretakers of the world. This isn't just ancient history; it's a living invitation. God is handing us the keys and saying, "Go ahead, I believe in you. Let's do this together!"

So how do we live out that promise?

We start by saying, **"Amen."**
God already said **"Yes."**
Now it's our turn to agree with Him.

Let's take a closer look at Matthew 9:20–22, where we meet a woman who had been suffering from bleeding for twelve long years. Her story shows us something powerful. Picture this: she hears that Jesus is healing people, and in verse 21 she muses, **"If I can just touch His robe, I will be healed."** Now imagine her repeating that to herself over and over as she pushes through the crowd to get to Him.

Here's the amazing part: when she finally touches His robe, Jesus turns around and says, **"Daughter, take courage. Your faith has healed you."** Just like that, bam, she's healed. It's a moment that changes everything.

But don't miss this: she wasn't just hoping. She was speaking her healing into existence. Her words, filled with faith, were like seeds planted on the way to Jesus. And the moment she reached out in faith, those words came alive. Our words are powerful when they're backed by faith.

The next time you're going through something hard, remember this woman, because what you say and believe matters. It's not wishful thinking; it's faith in action. And like her, your faith-filled words might be the very key to your breakthrough.

Now, let's go back to the Old Testament. There, we see God making promises to His people, promises of protection, provision, and His never-ending presence. From His covenant with Abraham, where He promised children as countless as the stars, to the rescue of His people from slavery in Exodus, we see one thing clearly: God always keeps His word. His promises are full of power, and His faithfulness never fails.

God always keeps His word. Every promise He makes will come true. Numbers 23:19 (NIV) says, **"God is not human, that He should lie, not a human being, that He should change His mind. Does He speak and then not act? Does He promise and not fulfill?"**

Now think about Joshua 14:9–12 (NIV), where Caleb holds on to a promise God gave him forty-five years earlier. In verse 9, he recalls: **"So on that day Moses swore to me, 'The land on which your feet have walked will be your**

inheritance and that of your children forever, because you have followed the Lord my God wholeheartedly.'"

Then in verse 12, Caleb boldly says, "Now give me this hill country that the Lord promised me that day..."

Caleb didn't let time shake his faith. He waited with trust, not disappointment. He kept saying "Yes and Amen" to the promise, believing it was still his. And after all those years, he stepped into his inheritance. His story proves that when we wait with faith, God's promises come alive. With a loud and faithful "Yes and Amen," Caleb stayed strong. His life shouts this truth: waiting in faith leads to the fulfillment of God's promises.

Now fast-forward to the New Testament, where God shows, once again, that He keeps His promises through Jesus Christ. It's like the grand finale of His love and commitment to us. The long-awaited Savior arrives, bringing salvation, forgiveness, and eternal life with Him.

Jesus promises peace, true rest, and a life full of meaning to anyone who chooses to follow Him. Imagine Him calling out in Matthew 11:28–30 (NIV): **"Come to me, all you who are weary and burdened, and I will give you rest."**

That's God's powerful "Yes" to every deep need we carry. And when we respond with our own "Amen," we step into the life He's always promised us.

Let's take a look at some of the powerful promises of God:

1. God promises you everlasting life.

> "For God so loved the world that He gave His only begotten Son, that whoever believes in Him should not perish but have everlasting life" (John 3:16, NKJV).

2. God promises that nothing can separate you from His love.

> "For I am convinced that neither death nor life, neither angels nor demons, neither the present nor the future, nor any powers, neither height nor depth, nor anything else in all creation will be able to separate us from the love of God that is in Christ Jesus our Lord" (Romans 8:38-39, NIV).

3. God promises to answer your prayers.

> "Ask and it will be given to you; seek and you will find; knock and the door will be opened to you" (Matthew 7:7, NIV).

4. God promises to work everything out for your good.

> "And we know that God causes everything to work together for the good of those who love God and are called according to His purpose for them" (Romans 8:28 NLT).

5. God promises to take care of all your needs.

> "And my God will meet all your needs according to the riches of His glory in Christ Jesus" (Philippians 4:19, NIV).

6. God promises to be with you.

> "Fear not, for I am with you; be not dismayed, for I am your God. I will strengthen you and help you; I will uphold you with My righteous right hand" (Isaiah 41:10, NKJV).

7. God promises to protect you.

> "He will call on Me, and I will answer him; I will be with him in trouble, I will deliver him and honor him" (Psalm 91:15, NIV).

8. God promises healing.

> "He Himself bore our sins in His body on the cross, so that we might die to sin and live for righteousness; by His wounds you have been healed" (1 Peter 2:24, NIV).

These promises aren't stories from long ago; they're alive and real today. When life gets hard, we can stand on these truths. We can hold tightly to His promises and boldly declare, **"Yes and Amen!"** God promises He will never leave us or forsake us (Hebrews 13:5). That gives us peace and courage in the middle of life's storms.

One of the most significant promises in the New Testament is the gift of the Holy Spirit. God promises to live in us, to guide us, comfort us, and give us strength for the journey of faith. That's a promise we can depend on every single day. He has all the wisdom and power to execute His promises for His children. We can see in Psalm 33:9 (NIV), **"For He spoke and it was done, He commanded and it stood fast."** Let that truth settle in your heart. God keeps His promises, and they are still unfolding in your life today.

Reflection Questions:

1. What does saying "Yes and Amen" mean to you personally? How does it affect the way you view God's promises?

2. Have you ever experienced the pain of a broken promise? How did that impact your trust in people, in yourself, or even in God?

3. How do you respond when a promise takes longer than expected? Are you waiting in faith or struggling with doubt?

4. Can you think of a time when you spoke words of faith like the woman with the issue of blood? What was the outcome? Did you sense God moving in that situation?

5. Which one of His promises means the most to you right now? Why does it speak to your heart?

6. What would it look like for you to say "Amen" today, through your words, your attitude, or your actions?

7. How are you allowing the Holy Spirit to lead you in this season of your life?

Closing Prayer:

Father God,

Thank You for being the Promise Keeper. Your Word never fails, and everything you speak is true. Even when life is uncertain, Your promises are my anchor. Help me to trust You like Caleb did, to wait patiently and wholeheartedly. Teach me to say "Yes and Amen" not just with my mouth, but with my life. Strengthen my faith when the wait is long. Fill me with Your Spirit, so I can walk in boldness and obedience, knowing You are faithful to fulfill every word You've spoken.

In Jesus' mighty name, Amen.

CHAPTER 7

The Power of Speaking Blessings

Life throws some brutal punches our way, especially when those close to us start slinging arrows of negativity, calling us fools, predicting our failure, and expressing frustration. These words don't carry the warmth of blessings; they feel more like curses.

When we're hit with discouraging and condemning words, it's like an arrow piercing deep into our souls. The emotional hurt often surpasses any physical pain we might feel. Words have this incredible power; they can tear a person down, silencing their voice. Let's navigate through this storm together and find the strength to rise above the destructive impact of hurtful words.

If you're going through a tough time right now, consider this: *speak blessings*. It might sound simple, but it's a powerful choice. Let's look at 1 Peter 3:9 (NLT): **"Don't repay evil for evil. Don't retaliate with insults when people**

insult you. Instead, pay them back with a blessing. That is what God has called you to do, and He will grant you His blessing."

This passage from 1 Peter advises against responding to negativity with more negativity. Instead, counter it with a blessing. Why? Because blessings are part of the promise God made to you when He called you. In conflict, choose to speak blessings to break free from the cycle of negativity and tap into the promise of God's goodness.

God urges us to bless those who curse us, a seemingly straightforward path yet immensely challenging. I've been there, navigating this tough journey a few years back. Sharp and bitter words, unexpectedly coming from someone I deeply respected, cut through me. The impact went beyond the surface, lingering in my soul for weeks. Despite my prayers and efforts to forgive and forget, the weight stayed with me day after day. Joy and peace seemed like distant friends, and my heart carried a heavy load. Emotions took over, and I felt trapped in a cycle of depression and anger towards them. Let's explore how to find healing and release the burden of resentment together.

I cried out to God, pleading for relief from my overwhelming feelings. That's when I encountered that word in 1 Peter 3 as a revelation that transformed my perspective. I realized that for my freedom, I needed to bless those who had wounded me. I prayed for them, forgave them, and purposefully spoke blessings over their lives. I asked the Lord to open their hearts to see others through the lens of Jesus Christ, offering grace and kindness. Slowly but surely, the weight started to lift. In its place, I received the peace and joy of God.

Reflecting on Luke 6:28, where Jesus Himself urges us to bless those who curse us and pray for those who mistreat us, I discovered a transformative power in choosing to respond with blessing. It's not an easy journey, but it leads to a profound sense of freedom and inner peace.

Moving forward, whenever I face challenges, I turn to my emergency "Gos-pill," (Word of God) found in 1 Peter 3:9. Speaking blessings holds power. In Christ, we are already loaded with blessings, as Ephesians 1:3 (NLT) reveals, **"All praise to God, the Father of our Lord Jesus Christ, who has blessed us with every spiritual blessing in the heavenly realms because we are united with Christ."** Blessings are not just words; they carry life and creative force.

> *"Count your blessings, not your troubles. Embrace each day as a gift and let positivity guide your way."* - **Roy T Bennett, Author of the book *The Light in the Heart*.**

From the very beginning, God's first words to Adam and Eve were words of blessing. **Then God blessed them, and God said to them, "Be fruitful and multiply; fill the earth and subdue it; have dominion over the fish of the sea, over the birds of the air, and over every living thing that moves on the earth"** Genesis 1:28 (NKJV). Even as Jesus ascended to Heaven, His last parting words to His disciples were words of blessing. **"And He led them out as far as Bethany, and He lifted His hands and blessed them. Now it came to pass, while He blessed them, that He was parted from them and carried up into heaven"** Luke 24:50-51 (NKJV). Blessing is woven into the fabric of God's heart for us.

God didn't just give Adam and Eve a command; He blessed them to be fruitful and multiply. He imparted to them the authority and the very power to reign over and subdue the earth. This act set a profound precedent. Even centuries later, just before Jesus ascended to Heaven, His final precious words to His disciples were not mandates, but words of blessing. This legacy continues, for we are inherently called to be a blessing to others. When you genuinely tell someone, "You are a blessing," or "Your presence is a blessing to me," the impact is immediate. These simple words don't just express gratitude; they fill the heart with a powerful sense of hope and deep encouragement. This became especially meaningful when I found myself silently struggling through discouragement and disappointment. Your affirmation can become a light in their darkness.

However, the enemy seeks to thwart God's blessings in our lives, attempting to steal the abundant blessings God has in store for us.

Let me share a story that still resonates with me, about my friend Reeja from a decade ago. Reeja was hurting, her heart shattered by the constant words of her spouse, belittling her and chipping away at her self-esteem. She grappled with her identity in Christ. And it led her to a dark place of depression and even thoughts about ending her life. In her job as a nurse, the weight of it all made her timid, unable to function.

When Reeja came to me seeking help, I pointed to the powerful truth in 1 Peter 3:9. I urged her to speak blessings over herself and her husband: "The blessing of the Lord is upon me, and it makes me rich in every area of my life. I am walking in the fullness of God's divine plan and purpose for me. God has blessed me with every spiritual blessing in heavenly places. I am a channel of blessing, and everything I touch prospers. My family and loved ones are blessed with peace, unity, and love. I am blessed with the wisdom to nurture and guide my children and family well. My home is a sanctuary of joy, grace, and harmony. I bless my loved ones with success and wholeness in every part of their lives."

It became a turning point in her life. Reeja began blessing every challenging situation. Whenever Reeja faced her husband's harsh words, she would answer by saying, "I forgive you. I love you. You are a blessing in my life." It was deeply painful at first. Yet she was consistent in her declarations. Her husband received her kindness and gradually stopped mistreating her. She continued speaking blessings over her kids, her spouse, her colleagues, and every patient she met. Picture this: she walked into each patient's room with a warm smile, leaving a blessing—spoken or written on the board— "You are blessed" or "Have a blessed day."

Blessing notes decorated her nurse's station, and she even spoke blessings over her staff.

The transformative power of blessing didn't just stop there. Reeja, once timid, depressed, and on the brink of despair, became a powerhouse of blessings. She turned from receiving to giving, encouraging everyone she met. She blesses her husband and her children every day with positive changes in their lives. Reeja pursued education, becoming a nurse practitioner. She started a clinic, a place where she can continue pouring out blessings on every patient who walks through the door. It's a testimony to the life-changing impact of the simple yet profound act of speaking blessings.

Check out this incredible blessing journey spanning generations! God gives Abraham the ultimate call to adventure: leave your hometown, family, and father's place, and I'll show you a new land. But here's the catch: God drops some revelatory promises: "You're gonna be a great nation. Blessings? Oh, they're coming your way. Your name? I will make your name great. Plus, every family on Earth? Yep, they're going to be blessed through you."

It's all in Genesis 12:1-3, a divine roadmap of blessings. Let's unpack this legacy and see how it's shaping our lives today. God blessed Abraham, and Abraham passed that blessing to Isaac. Isaac, in turn, blessed Jacob, who in turn blessed all his descendants. We, too, are beneficiaries of the Abrahamic Covenant of blessing. We are blessed to be a blessing to others.

Dive into the beautiful priestly blessings tucked away in Numbers 6:24-26 (NLT), they're like a heavenly blueprint for Godly favor. **"May the Lord bless you and protect you. May the Lord smile on you and be gracious to you. May the Lord show you His favor and give you His peace."** Imagine these words were a direct blessing from God to Moses, Aaron, and their sons, meant to shower the Israelites with divine goodness.

Did you know that even today, Jewish families keep up the tradition of blessing their children? It's pretty incredible. Despite facing discrimination worldwide, people of Jewish faith or lineage continue to be a blessing to the world. Think about it, countless Jewish scientists, composers, educators, and artists, and other professionals have poured their talents into enriching all of humanity. It's like a living testament to the enduring power of blessing and resilience.

Now, here's the exciting part: claiming that same blessing, those very words spoken by God, for yourself and your loved ones. It's like tapping into a treasure chest of heavenly goodness waiting to unfold in your life. Let's explore how this ancient blessing can bring a fresh wave of God's favor into your journey.

God's Blessings to Multiply

God's all about multiplication, and it's not only a math thing. He blessed Adam and Eve, then told them to go ahead, be fruitful, multiply, and rule the earth.

Now, let's fast forward to Jesus, the ultimate multiplier. Picture this: five loaves of bread and two fish. Sounds like a light snack, right? But hold on, in Matthew 14:19-21, Jesus turns this little meal into a feast for 5000. He tells the crowd to take a seat, then He looks up to heaven, gives those loaves and fish a divine blessing, breaks them, and hands them over to His disciples, who pass them on to the hungry crowd.

It's like a heavenly potluck where Jesus takes the little we have, blesses it, and turns it into a feast of abundance. So, what's the takeaway? God's into multiplication, not just with bread and fish but with our lives too. His blessings can multiply in your journey, turning the ordinary into the extraordinary.

Here's a little tale about the power of blessing food. I'm at a prayer gathering, and out of the blue, a bunch of unexpected guests roll in. Panic mode, right? That's when it hits me, let's bless the food. So, I go ahead and pray, asking for God's provision. We not only had enough for everyone, but we also ended up with leftovers. It's like a simple prayer turned into a feast of abundance.

God's Heart to Bless Children

God shows His heart when it comes to blessing children in Mark 10:14-16 (NIV). Jesus saw His disciples trying to prevent children from coming to Him. And oh boy, he became upset and said to them, **"Let the little children come to me, do not hinder them, for the kingdom of God**

belongs to such as these... And he took the children in his arms, placed His hands on them and blessed them."

Now, here's the best part: Jesus isn't just talking. He scoops up those little ones, wraps them in His arms, lays His hands on their heads, and showers them with blessings. He's saying, "Look, the kingdom of God? It's for the childlike hearts, the ones who trust, wonder, and soak in goodness without overthinking it."

> "Today, choose to be a source of kindness and love. Let your actions create ripples of blessings throughout the day." – Mimi Novic, Inspirational author and motivational speaker

So, what's the lesson for us? Have childlike faith, embrace the simplicity, and let God's blessings rain down on us. Doing so is a divine hug for our souls, and who wouldn't want a piece of that? Let's explore how to tap into God's heart for blessings, especially when we're feeling a bit too grown-up for our good.

God's double portion blessings:

Let's talk about God's double dose of blessings. It's a real game-changer. Job, who we read about in the Old Testament book that bears his name, is right smack in the middle of a storm. His life is a wreck, all his children are gone, his property is destroyed, his health fails, and even his wife turns against him. But here's the powerful part:

after Job endures the storm and holds on to his faith, God shows up. They share a deep, honest conversation, and Job's understanding of who God is deepens, becoming more personal than ever before.

Now, here's where it gets really cool. Instead of wallowing in self-pity, Job does something remarkable. He prays for his friends. And guess what? God doesn't just restore what the enemy stole; He goes above and beyond, handing Job a double portion of blessings.

So, what's the takeaway? God's into restoration, and when we stay strong in the storm and bless others, He's ready to unleash a double dose of goodness in our lives. Let's unpack how this ancient story can breathe fresh hope into your challenges and bring a double portion of God's blessings into your journey.

> **"When we lose one blessing, another is often most unexpectedly given in its place." - C.S. Lewis, from a collection of letters titled *Letters to an American Lady*.**

This chapter beautifully reminds us that our words hold spiritual weight, either building or breaking, healing, or harming. In a world where negative voices echo loudly, God calls His children to be a different sound, to speak blessings, not bitterness.

When we are hurt, our natural tendency may not be to respond in kind. But Scripture, especially 1 Peter 3:9 and Luke 6:28, flips that script. God invites us to participate in something far greater than retaliation; He invites us into restoration through blessing. This is not weakness; it is warfare. When we bless those who curse us, we disarm the enemy's weapons and release heaven's power.

Your stories and Reeja's journey are living proof that blessing changes not only atmospheres but also hearts, homes, and destinies. Blessing breaks chains of depression, bitterness, and self-doubt. Speaking life is a divine partnership with the Holy Spirit, who breathes on our words and multiplies their impact, just like Jesus multiplied the loaves and fish.

You don't need the perfect words. You need a willing heart. As you bless, God multiplies. As you speak life, His Spirit moves. And as you walk in His Word, the legacy of blessing continues through you. Blessing isn't reserved for the "super spiritual." It's for all of us, mothers, fathers, teachers, doctors, friends, and believers of every kind. We have inherited the blessing of Abraham, and now we are called to be a blessing to others.

Reflection Questions:

1. How can you incorporate the practice of speaking blessings into your daily life, especially in challenging situations?

2. In times of conflict or hurtful words, how can you emulate the example of blessing others as outlined in the stories shared in this chapter?

3. What blessings from Scripture, such as those found in Numbers 6:24-26, can you incorporate into your prayers for yourself and those around you?

Closing Prayer:

Heavenly Father,

Thank You for blessing us with every spiritual blessing in Christ. You have called us not to repay evil with evil, but to release blessings, even when it's hard. Teach us to speak words that heal, words that lift, and words that reflect Your heart. When we are tempted to curse, give us grace to bless. When we feel broken, remind us to bless ourselves with Your truth. Let our mouths be fountains of encouragement, love, and life. Make us bold like Jesus, tender like Jesus, and full of compassion like Jesus.

May the words we speak sow seeds of peace and bear fruit that remains. And may we never forget we are blessed to be a blessing.

In Jesus' name,
Amen.

CHAPTER 8

Overcoming Your Obstacles

> **"Obstacles are those frightful things you see when you take your eyes off your goal." - Henry Ford, President of Ford Motor Company**

Have you ever felt like everyone else is moving forward while you're stuck in the same place? You pray, you fast, but still feel like nothing is changing. It can be so frustrating to see others doing well while you're left wondering why God isn't pouring out His blessings on you.

But here's the truth: God isn't holding back blessings from you. Many times, we are the ones blocking them. Yes, that's right. Often, the roadblocks in our lives come from us. We need to take a closer look inside our hearts, check what we believe, and pay attention to the words we speak.

Imagine a life full of blessings, where your prayers are answered, and good things come your way. That kind of life is possible! But first, we must remove the things that stand in the way. It's time to search our hearts, break free from the barriers we've created, and receive the blessings God already wants to give us.

Deuteronomy 30:19 (NLT) says it clearly: **"Today, I have given you the choice between life and death, between blessings or curses. Now I call heaven and earth to witness the choice you make. Oh, that you would choose life, so that you and your descendants might live."** God has given us the power to decide. Will we choose words and actions that bring blessings, or those that bring trouble?

When we speak positively, it's like setting our lives on the right path. Your journey becomes one filled with purpose, and your children are blessed, too. Peace and joy follow you when your words line up with God's truth. But if your words are full of fear, doubt, or anger, it's like driving into a never-ending traffic jam. Everything feels stuck. Joy and peace fade away, and frustration takes their place. That's not the life God wants for you.

1 Peter 3:10 (NLT) gives us this advice: **"If you want to enjoy life and see many happy days, keep your tongue from speaking evil and your lips from telling lies."** Your words have power. They can bring life or bring harm. So, speak with care. The words you choose do shape your future.

Let me tell you about my friend, Alaina. She constantly speaks fear and failure over her life. Ever since she got married, she says it's like her life has hit a wall. She's been praying and fasting, asking God to help her family grow in faith and be blessed, but nothing seems to be happening. She feels completely worn out and hopeless.

She tells me that her children aren't becoming the people she dreamed they would be. She keeps comparing them to other kids, and it breaks her heart. She also carries deep frustration and hurt toward her husband because he's not leading their family spiritually the way she hoped. Even though I gently remind her to speak with faith and choose her words wisely, she keeps repeating the same painful story, as if she's stuck in a loop.

Now she feels trapped and surrounded by anger, sadness, and doubt. Some days, she even wonders if God can still hear her cries. Here's the truth: When we keep thinking about our past mistakes and painful moments, we're permitting them to follow us around. We're letting those memories control our thoughts and emotions. In doing that, we unknowingly give the enemy power over our faith.

Proverbs 18:21 (NIV) puts it clearly: **"The tongue has the power of life and death, and those who love it will eat its fruit."** What we say matters. Our spoken words are a double-edged sword: they can cut down or build up. Words create our reality: heaven or hell. With our tongue, we author our triumph or our tragedy. The tongue is a flame that warms or consumes.

Isaiah 43:18-19 (NIV) encourages us to **"forget the former things; do not dwell on the past"** because God is doing **"a new thing!"** and it is making a way even in diffi-cult circumstances.

This concept is reinforced in Philippians 3:13-14 (NIV): **"Brothers and sisters, I do not consider myself yet to have taken hold of it. But one thing I do: Forgetting what is behind and straining toward what is ahead, I press on toward the goal to win the prize for which God has called me heavenward in Christ Jesus."** Apostle Paul speaks of "forgetting what is behind and straining toward what is ahead."

These verses highlight the idea of moving forward, leaving behind past hurts, mistakes, and failures, to embrace the new things God has in store for us.

And Isaiah 59:2 (NIV) gives us a potent reminder: **"But your iniquities have separated you from your God; your sins have hidden His face from you, so that He will not hear."** That's serious. Sin doesn't just hurt us; it also creates distance between the Lord and us.

This may sound hard, but it's a loving warning. It's God's way of urging us to be more careful with the words we speak.

Let's be wise and choose to be intentional with words of life, hope, and truth. With God's help, we can break free from the old cycle and move forward in faith.

Now, let's talk about a few things that might be blocking blessings in your life:

1. Unforgiveness and bitterness:
Holding on to bitterness and refusing to forgive is like slamming the door shut on God's blessings. Jesus makes it clear in Matthew 6:14-15 (NIV), **"For if you forgive other people when they sin against you, your Heavenly Father will also forgive you. But if you do not forgive others their sins, your Father will not forgive your sins."**

Imagine Jesus hanging on the Cross, held there by three nails. His body was in unbearable pain, and He was desperately thirsty. Yet, even in that suffering, He looked down at the soldiers who mocked and hurt Him, and He didn't respond with anger or hate. Instead, He looked up to His Father in heaven and prayed, "Father, forgive them, for they don't know what they're doing."

In that moment, Jesus prayed for the very people who were causing Him pain. He gave His life on the Cross to pay the price for our sins past, present, and future. He took on our sins, sickness, our brokenness, and our burdens. And as He breathed His last breath, He said,

"It is finished."

He completed the greatest act of love and forgiveness the world has ever known.

If Jesus could forgive so completely, even while suffering so deeply, then we can take a step toward forgiveness too.

Let go of the pain you've been carrying. Say the names of those who hurt you and choose to speak forgiveness for each one of them aloud, just as Jesus forgave you.

When you do, you make room in your heart for peace, healing, and blessing.

Forgiveness doesn't change the past, but it opens the door to a freer, lighter future.

2. Anger and Rage:

Uncontrolled anger and rage can become spiritual roadblocks that stop us from fully receiving the blessings God wants to give us. When anger is left unresolved, it can damage our relationships, not only with other people but also with God. This kind of anger can make it hard to feel His peace or hear His voice. It may also cause problems in our communication with both God and others, and it might even block what God wants to do through us or in the lives of those around us.

When we let anger sit in our hearts, it often grows into bitterness and resentment. That creates a spiritual wall between God and us, and it can hurt our prayer life. We may start to feel distant from God, like His presence has faded, even though He never leaves us. Anger that goes unchecked often shows up in harmful ways. We may say cruel things, act in revenge, or lash out at others. These actions not only hurt people but also open the door to sin. A young couple came to my office seeking marriage counseling. I began by speaking with the wife privately.

She shared that her husband frequently displays anger and exhibits controlling behavior. She described living in a constant state of anxiety, feeling as though she had to walk on eggshells to avoid triggering his outbursts. She also expressed fear that the situation could escalate to physical harm. She explained that she was seeking counseling for emotional healing, as she felt she had lost her sense of identity and no longer had a voice due to her husband's ongoing verbal abuse.

When I invited her husband in for his portion of the session, he quickly became defensive. As I began to ask questions, he stood up abruptly and demanded, "Who are you?" I responded, "I'm a Christian counselor." He replied angrily, "I didn't come here to see a counselor. I came to meet with a mediator to sign divorce papers." The wife had not fully disclosed the purpose of the visit to him, hoping to save the marriage. Feeling misled, he became upset, lashed out, and left the office.

Holding on to anger affects us in every area, physically, emotionally, and spiritually. Anger is often tied to unforgiveness. But Jesus taught us how important forgiveness is in Matthew 6:14–15. If we forgive others, God forgives us. If we don't, it affects our relationship with Him. In Ephesians 4:26–27 (NKJV), we are told, **"Be angry and do not sin," do not let the sun go down on your wrath, nor give place to the devil."** This shows that feeling anger isn't wrong, but letting it control us is. Proverbs 14:29 reminds us that wise people are patient and slow to anger, underscoring the importance of self-control. Colossians 3:13 tells us to forgive others just as God forgives us. When we forgive, we let go of the heavy burden of anger and open the door to healing and restoration.

The wife began attending counseling sessions on her own for a few weeks. Eventually, her husband agreed to join her. Through the sessions, God revealed the root of his anger. After some time, he reconciled with his wife.

In short, when anger is not dealt with, it becomes a serious spiritual problem. It blocks God's blessings, disrupts our connection with Him, and harms our well-being. But when we bring our anger to God through prayer, ask for His help to forgive, and follow His Word, we begin to grow spiritually. We also start to live in His peace and walk more fully in the blessings He has for us.

3. Being Judgmental and critical:

Have you ever caught yourself being critical or judgmental? It comes more naturally than we think. It involves jumping to conclusions based on personal values or biases, often without acknowledging other reasons or factors. But that attitude can actually block the blessings God wants to give us. Jesus warns in Matthew 7:1-2 (NIV): **"Do not judge, or you too will be judged. For in the same way you judge others, you will be judged, and with the measure you use, it'll be measured to you."**

When we judge others, it's like we set a trap for ourselves. It creates tension, bitterness, and even pride. Romans 14:10,

13 (NLT) reminds us: **"So why do you condemn another believer? Why do you look down on another believer? Remember, we will all stand before the judgment seat of God... So, let's stop condemning each other. Decide instead to live in such a way that you will not cause another believer to stumble and fall."**

So, instead of judging, let's correct in love. Speaking the truth with grace can clear the way for blessings and bring peace both to you and those around you.

4. Doubt:

Have you ever prayed and believed for something, only to have that belief fade over time? It's a common struggle. Waiting can be hard, especially when answers don't come right away. That's when fear and discouragement sneak in and shake our faith.

Remember Abraham? God promised him a child, but it didn't happen right away. His wife, Sarah, suggested they take matters into their own hands by having a child through her servant Hagar. That decision brought a lot of trouble. Sometimes shortcuts cost more than patience.

James 1:6-8 (NIV) says it clearly: **"But when you ask, you must believe and not doubt, because the one who doubts is like a wave of the sea, blown and tossed by the wind. That person should not expect to receive anything from the Lord. Such a person is double-minded and unstable in all they do."**

Romans 4:19-20 (NLT): **"And Abraham's faith did not weaken, even though at about 100 years of age, he figured his body was as good as dead– and so was Sarah's womb. Abraham never wavered in believing God's promise. In fact, his faith grew stronger, and in this he brought glory to God."**

Abraham learned to trust God's timing. Even when it looked impossible, he chose to believe. And at 100 years old, he finally received the promised son. His faith was counted as righteous. The lesson? Don't let doubt steal the blessing that's already on the way.

About ten years ago, my husband started a pharmacy business. The beginning was rough. When people asked how it was going, he would honestly say, "It's not doing well." And the truth was, we were struggling, financially, emotionally, and spiritually. It was a hard season. But something shifted when my husband made a bold choice. Instead of talking about failure, he started declaring blessings over the pharmacy. Every day, he spoke life and faith into that business, even when nothing had changed.

Then something amazing happened. After a few months of speaking blessings, the business started to turn around. We went from loss to growth. The income increased. And when people asked how the company was doing, he could joyfully say, "It's going very well!"

The words he spoke carried power and invited God's blessing to come in and do what only He can do.

5. The Snare of Pride:

Be careful of falling into the trap of pride and an unrepentant heart. Pride leads to bragging and sarcasm, blocking the blessings of God. It blinds us from seeing our own mistakes and makes it hard to say, "I was wrong." Instead of taking responsibility, we blame others. This creates conflict and keeps us stuck.

We can see the consequences of pride in the following scriptures:

> Proverbs 16:18 (NKJV) "Pride goes before destruction, and a haughty spirit before a fall."
>
> James 4:6 (NIV) "...God opposes the proud but shows favor to the humble."
>
> Proverbs 29:23 (NIV) "Pride brings a person low, but the lowly in spirit gain honor."
>
> Matthew 23:12 (NKJV) "And whoever exalts himself will be humbled, and he who humbles himself will be exalted."

Matthew 12:37 (NKJV) says clearly, **"For by your words you will be justified, and by your words you will be condemned."** What we say matters. The power of our words is undeniable, and what we voice has a tangible impact on our future.

1 John 1:8 (NKJV) reminds us, **"If we say that we have no sin, we deceive ourselves, and the truth is not in us."** It is important that we first admit our sins and humble ourselves before Him.

Thankfully, 1 John 1:9 (NKJV) shows us the way forward: **"If we confess our sins, He is faithful and just to forgive us our sins and to cleanse us from all unrighteousness."** This is a promise of God's grace when we come to Him with honest repentance.

1 Peter 5:5 (NIV) also gives great advice: **"... All of you, clothe yourselves with humility toward one another, because God opposes the proud but shows favor to the humble."** Pride pushes God away, but humility draws Him near. We must choose humility in both our words and our actions.

6. Fear, Worry, and Anxiety

Have you ever felt trapped by fear and worry, so overwhelmed that even daily life feels too hard? It's like being stuck in a storm, unable to think clearly or move forward. Anxiety takes control, turning simple tasks into significant challenges. Fear sneaks in quietly, stealing your peace and joy, and replacing them with constant worry.

Thomas D. Wilhite (Air Force General) says, *"Worry never accomplishes anything. When you have a problem, it is best to concentrate on the solution to that problem, not the problem itself."*

There was a season in my life when anxiety filled every corner of my days. I worried about everything: my health, my children's safety, and our future. The fear grew so strong that it began to control me. I found myself constantly saying, "I can't do it because..." Simple things felt overwhelming.

I couldn't even sleep peacefully whenever my husband was out of town. During those difficult nights, I prayed sometimes with desperation, sometimes with quiet hope. And in that place of seeking, God led me to a seminar at Above and Beyond Christian Counseling. That was the turning point, the moment I began to break free from the grip of fear and anxiety.

From then on, every time fear and anxiety tried to creep in again, I chose to fight back. I resisted the spirit of fear and anxiety and declared the Scriptures aloud over and over until peace returned.

2 Timothy 1:7 (NKJV) became a strong foundation for me: **"For God has not given us a spirit of fear, but of power and of love and of a sound mind."**

Psalm 27:1 (NKJV) also gave me comfort: **"The Lord is my light and my salvation, whom shall I fear? The Lord is the strength of my life, of whom shall I be afraid?"**

7. Guilt, Shame, and Condemnation

Guilt, shame, and condemnation are heavy burdens that block the power of God in our lives. When we carry the weight of past mistakes, it clouds our view of God's grace and mercy. This is one of the enemy's favorite tricks: to keep us trapped in our past.

I still remember the weight of guilt and shame in my life, pushing me into the dark realm of condemnation. I felt distant from God, drowning in the pain of anger and rejection. It all started with a back injury at work, and my husband, wanting to help, took me to a massage therapist whom he trusted. As he left the room, this therapist overstepped boundaries, massaging me against my will. He was not supposed to leave the room. The fear of my husband's reaction towards the therapist silenced me for days.

The anger toward my husband (for not being there), the therapist, and myself became an unbearable burden. I felt like I failed God and myself. I asked myself why I hadn't screamed or yelled at the moment. The emotional pain ran so deep that I resorted to pulling my hair to cope. Finally, I found the courage to break the silence and tell my husband about the violation. His love and the words of God helped me heal from the emotional pain. I chose to forgive the therapist, and to forgive my husband for leaving me alone in the room, and most importantly, I forgave myself, finding healing through love and God's grace.

Romans 8:1-3 (NIV) tells us: **"Therefore, there is now no condemnation for those who are in Christ Jesus, because through Christ Jesus the law of the Spirit who gives life has set you free from the law of sin and death. For what the law was powerless to do because it was weakened by the flesh. God did by sending His own Son in the likeness of sinful flesh to be a sin offering. And so He condemned sin in the flesh."**

When you repent sincerely, you are no longer condemned. If guilt and shame keep coming back, it may be the voice of the enemy trying to pull you back into darkness. But James

4:7 (NIV) gives us power: **"Submit yourselves, then, to God. Resist the devil, and he will flee from you."**

We are free in Christ. In Him, guilt and shame have no place. This journey is about learning who we are in Christ, repenting when we fall short, and walking boldly in the freedom He gives. When we speak words filled with faith, love, and truth, we invite God's blessings into our lives and the lives of those around us.

The key lies in choosing life-affirming words, aligning our speech with God's truth, and breaking free from the chains that hinder the free flow of blessings into our lives. The journey is one of self-discovery, repentance, and embracing the freedom found in Christ. May we, as believers, continually choose words that reflect His grace, love, and power, unlocking the abundant blessings that await us.

Reflection Questions:

1. What obstacles in your life might be coming from your own words, thoughts, or attitudes rather than from outside circumstances?

2. In what areas have you allowed unforgiveness or bitterness to take root, and how is it affecting your relationship with God and others?

3. Is anger or unresolved hurt influencing the way you respond to others? How is it blocking peace or progress in your life?

4. Where have you struggled with judging or criticizing others, and how can you shift toward responding with grace and understanding?

5. What promises has God given you that you've begun to doubt? How can you renew your faith in His timing?

6. Is pride keeping you from admitting wrongs, apologizing, or seeking forgiveness? What step toward humility can you take today?

7. What fears or worries have been controlling your decisions, and what truth from God's Word can you hold onto to break their power?

8. What past guilt or shame do you need to release so you can fully receive God's forgiveness and walk in freedom?

9. What "life-giving" words can you intentionally begin speaking over yourself, your family, or your circumstances this week?

Closing Prayer:

Heavenly Father,

Thank You for revealing the truth through this chapter. We acknowledge the times we've allowed fear, pride, and unforgiveness to block Your blessings. Cleanse our hearts, renew our minds, and help us release every burden we've been carrying.

Lord, teach us to speak life and not defeat. Let our words reflect Your truth and our hearts align with Your will. Break every cycle that keeps us stuck and let Your healing flow freely.

Help us to walk in humility, live in faith, and trust that You are working all things for our good. We declare that obstacles are falling, and breakthrough has begun.

In Jesus' name,
Amen.

CHAPTER 9

The Creative Power of Your Tongue

Your tongue has the power to change the course of your life, for better or for worse. The words you speak can shape your future. When you speak words in faith that line up with God's Word, you release the creative power of God inside you. That power builds, strengthens, and brings growth. But when you speak in fear and doubt, you're agreeing with the voice of the enemy. That also releases creative power, but one that leads to disbelief, anxiety, and destruction.

Let's look at how the creative power of your tongue impacts three critical areas of your life:

1. The Creative Power of Your Tongue Over Health

The Bible teaches us that our words aren't only sounds; they are powerful tools for creation. When we speak words of healing and faith, we're not just talking; we're partnering with God and His promises. This doesn't mean we ignore sickness; it means we focus on God's power instead of the diagnosis, prognosis, and fear. We take responsibility for what comes out of our mouths and choose to expect healing, not defeat.

I remember back in 2003, I was getting ready to drive and pick up my children from school. As I was about to get into the car, I suddenly felt dizzy. I didn't feel safe driving. So, I called someone to drive me as I rested in the passenger seat. When I came back home, something felt terribly wrong. I couldn't get up from my seat. My body from the waist down felt weak, paralyzed. I was rushed to the hospital, and after a whole week of tests and examinations, the doctors found nothing wrong. Still, I couldn't walk.

I was devastated. I was a young mother, and my children needed me. But I couldn't even stand. My husband had to carry me for my personal needs. I had never felt so lost and hopeless.

Then I remembered a coworker who had been paralyzed and in a wheelchair for ten years. She was miraculously cured through a healing ministry. That gave me hope. I decided to fight back with faith. I began speaking healing scriptures over myself every single day.

I held on tightly to this promise from Isaiah 53:5 (KJV): **"But He was wounded for our transgressions; He was bruised for our iniquities; the chastisement of our peace was upon Him, and with His stripes we are healed."**

I also declared:

> Psalm 18:32–33 (NIV): "It is God who arms me with strength and keeps my way secure. He makes my feet like the feet of a deer; He causes me to stand on the heights."
>
> Habakkuk 3:19 (NIV): "The Sovereign Lord is my strength; He makes my feet like the feet of a deer, He enables me to tread on the heights."
>
> Malachi 4:2 (NLT): "But for you who fear My name, the Sun of Righteousness will rise with healing in His wings. And you will go free, leaping with joy like calves let out to pasture."

Every time I recited these scriptures, I would imagine God healing my back, hips, and legs. I would try to stand, holding onto something with all the strength I had. I would fall back into the chair. Then I'd do it again, and again. This went on for almost two months.

Then one day, something changed. I stood up. Like a child taking their first step, my legs were shaking, and tears poured down my face. I was overwhelmed with joy. I kept thanking God for giving me the strength to stand. Each day, I stood a little longer. Then I took one small step. It was shaky, but it was a step. I kept going. I walked like a baby, one step at a time. And finally, I could walk again.

Yes, there were moments when I felt afraid and full of doubt. But I made a choice: I would not give in to fear. I refused to let unbelief rule my heart. I kept speaking the

Word of God until His promises came alive in my body. Praise God for His healing power. Romans 4:19–24 (NLT) says: **"And Abraham's faith did not weaken, even though, at about 100 years of age, he figured his body was as good as dead, and so was Sarah's womb. Abraham never wavered in believing God's promise. In fact, his faith grew stronger, and in this, he brought glory to God. He was fully convinced that God is able to do whatever He promises. And because of Abraham's faith, God counted him as righteous. And when God counted him as righteous, it wasn't just for Abraham's benefit. It was recorded for our benefit, too, assuring us that God will also count us righteous if we believe in Him, the One who raised Jesus our Lord from the dead."**

Important Points to Keep in Mind:
A. Daily Confession of Scriptures:
Speak the Word of God aloud every day. Declare His promises of healing and health. For example:

> "...By His wounds we are healed" Isaiah 53:5 (NIV).
>
> "Christ redeemed us from the curse of the law..." Galatians 3:13 (NIV).
>
> "So you shall serve the Lord your God, and He will bless your bread and your water. And I will take sickness away from the midst of you" (Exodus 23:25, NKJV).

B. Speak to Your Body:

Instead of talking about how sick you feel, speak to your body and command it to line up with God's truth. Say things like: "Spirit of infirmity, I rebuke you in Jesus' name." "Body, you are the temple of the Holy Spirit. You are strong and healthy!" "Pain, you must leave in the name of Jesus!"

C. Refuse Negative Confessions:

Be careful not to speak words that agree with sickness or give it power. Don't say, "I have a terrible illness." Instead, say, "I'm overcoming this sickness by God's power," or "The Lord is my Healer."

Remember what Proverbs 18:21 (NKJV) says: **"Death and life are in the power of the tongue..."** Your words matter. Don't give the enemy permission through negative speech.

D. Faith-Filled Declaration:

The words you speak are an expression of your faith. Power doesn't come from just saying words; it comes from the faith you release when you speak them. These words are how you show that you believe God's promises are real, even before you see the results. Because faith speaks. And when faith speaks, mountains move.

Healed from Food Intolerance and Food Sensitivity

The power of our words can change lives. One of my friends had been struggling for months with severe food sensitivities and intolerances. She could barely eat anything "normal." We attended a conference together and shared a room. When I saw her carrying a massive container of special water because she couldn't drink regular water, my heart sank. She told me how doctor after doctor, nutritionist after nutritionist, kept adding more foods to her "avoid" list.

In my spirit, I knew the enemy was targeting someone who is such a precious asset to the Kingdom of God. I asked if I could visit her at work to pray with her. When I arrived, she showed me pages, literally pages of foods she wasn't allowed to eat. I gently took the list from her and dropped it into the trash.

I told her, "You've been eating from the Tree of the Knowledge of Good and Evil. It's time to eat from the Tree of Life. The Tree of Life will heal you." The moment she heard those words, her faith ignited. She believed God was about to heal her.

We prayed. And God healed her completely. That very evening, she ate a full regular meal, and nothing happened. Since then, she has eaten everything with no restrictions. She no longer needs special water; she drinks regular water like everyone else. Praise the Lord!

Healing from Gluten Sensitivity

In 2022, I attended a women's conference with some friends from church. One morning, I went down for breakfast and noticed one of my dear friends standing in front of the beautifully arranged tables, simply staring at all the food. She wasn't picking up a single thing.

I asked, "What's wrong? Aren't you going to eat?" She sighed and said, "None of this is gluten-free. I don't think I can eat anything." At that moment, something rose in me. I told her, "We're going to pray, and you will eat. You're being healed from gluten sensitivity today." We prayed right there, and she ate breakfast. She has been completely healed from gluten sensitivity ever since. Hallelujah! Glory to God.

2. The Creative Power of Your Tongue Over Finances

When you face financial lack, what do you speak?

You can recognize that the world economy often moves with the nation's leader's declarations. You notice how the global stock market rises or falls based on a president's words. This shows that a word spoken with authority can instantly shift finances upward or downward. If the word of a simple human can influence the world economy within moments, imagine how powerful it becomes when you boldly speak the living WORD of the Creator who shaped the universe.

I remember my husband and I experiencing a hard season early in our marriage. Our son was two years old when I injured my back at work while lifting a patient. The doctor said I had a herniated disc and needed surgery. I was supposed to receive disability income until I recovered, but the claim was denied. They said it was a pre-existing condition. I'll never forget the moment my husband came home, placed a gallon of milk on the table, and then laid a single quarter beside it. He said, "This is all we have." I could see the pain and stress in his eyes.

There had been no income for nine months because my husband was still in pharmacy school. All I could see, feel, and speak was financial lack, sickness, and fear. I worried he wouldn't finish school. I was overwhelmed with hopelessness, anxiety, and both physical and emotional pain. It felt like a mighty army was marching toward me, getting closer every day. I would cry and pray, not knowing what to do or where to turn.

One day, a close family friend called to check on me. I shared all my fears about our future. He listened, prayed with me over the phone, and then asked me to read 2 Chronicles 20:1–30. He said, "Read it until the Holy Spirit meets you." I read it a few times and felt nothing, but I pushed through and read it one more time.

Then, something caught my attention: when the people began to worship, God Himself set an ambush against the enemy army coming to attack King Jehoshaphat. The King didn't have to fight at all. God won the battle. That truth hit my heart like a spark. My spirit woke up. I stopped complaining and started to worship, despite my intense back pain. I began speaking healing and provision scriptures over my life every day for a week:

> "And My God shall supply all your needs according to His riches in glory by Christ Jesus" Philippians 4:19 (NKJV).

> "The Lord is my Shepherd; I shall not want" Psalm 23:1 (NKJV).
>
> "The young lions lack and suffer hunger, but those who seek the Lord shall not lack any good thing" Psalm 34:10 (NKJV).
>
> "Praise the Lord, my soul, and forget not all His benefits, who forgives all your sins and heals all your diseases... who satisfies your desires with good things so that your youth is renewed like the eagle's." Psalm 103:2–5 (NIV).

After one week of worshiping in this manner, I opened the mailbox and found a check for the entire nine months of back pay for disability. Praise God! What was delayed for so long was released in a moment. The Lord fought the battle for me when I chose to worship Him. My faith grew so much that I fasted and prayed for three days, asking God to heal my back. And He did! I went back to work, healed and full of gratitude.

"And you will also declare a thing, and it will be established for you; so light will shine on your ways" (Job 22:28 NKJV). Keep declaring in faith and watch what God does for you.

A few years ago, there was a dentist who opened a clinic in Texas. She was full of faith and began declaring the Word that, **"Every good gift and every perfect gift is from above, and comes down from the Father of lights..."** James 1:17 (NKJV). She also declared, "My Heavenly Father only gives me good gifts, nothing bad. Let patients come to this clinic from the north, south, east, and west!" Over time, this clinic grew to be one of the busiest in town and even more so than some clinics that were established for much longer!

The creative power of your words over finances is not just about positive thinking. It's a spiritual discipline, grounded in faith in God's promises. The words themselves aren't magic; they're vessels that carry the power of the Holy Spirit and the authority of God's truth to bring about His will in your life.

3. The Creative Power of Your Tongue Over Nature

God created the entire universe by speaking. In Genesis 1, the phrase "And God said... Let there be..." is repeated again and again. It shows us the creative power of God's spoken word. Then, when God created humanity, He gave us dominion over the earth (Genesis 1:28). This authority wasn't meant to be passive; it's meant to be active, lived out through both our actions and our words. The power of the tongue is an extension of the dominion God gave us.

Jesus Calming the Storm

We see this power clearly when Jesus calmed the storm, a story recorded in Matthew, Mark, and Luke. After a long day of teaching, Jesus and His disciples were sailing across a lake when a violent storm suddenly hit. Waves crashed, the wind howled, and the boat seemed like it might sink.

In fear, the disciples woke Jesus, who had been sleeping. Jesus stood up, rebuked the wind and waves, and simply said, "Peace, be still." Instantly, the storm stopped. The disciples were amazed and even asked, "Who is this, that even the wind and waves obey Him?"

Just like Jesus spoke to the storm, we can speak to the storms in our own lives. Whether they are physical storms or emotional ones, we don't have to stay silent. Jesus, the Hope of Glory, lives inside of us. And He said in John 14:12 (NLT), **"I tell you the truth, anyone who believes in me will do the same works I have done, and even greater works, because I am going to be with the Father."**

I remember hearing about a wildfire that broke out in Colorado Springs. Everyone in a particular neighborhood was ordered to evacuate. My friend Debbie and her husband also got the order. But before they left, Debbie boldly declared, "No fire will come near my property in Jesus' name. I plead the blood of Jesus around my property line. Fire, you cannot cross that line!"

When they returned, they found that nearly every home around them had been destroyed by the fire, except for theirs. Not a single part of their house had been touched. That story stirred something deep in me. This made me understand the incredible power that comes from speaking with faith.

In October 2024, when Hurricane Milton hit parts of Florida, I remembered Debbie's story. The winds were fierce, and the warnings were everywhere. But I stood in faith and declared, "No harm will come to our home or our state in Jesus' name." I even spoke to the electric pole standing just behind our fence. I pointed at it and said, "You will stand firm. You will not move to the left or the right."

That night, the storm was terrifying. I heard loud crashes outside and thought for sure the pole had fallen. But when I looked out the next morning, the electric pole was still standing straight and strong. Trees behind it had fallen, but not a single branch in our yard was broken. God had protected everything we prayed for.

We did lose power during the storm. On the third day, I lifted my voice and prayed, "Lord, thank You for restoring our power before 1:00 p.m." Sure enough, at exactly 12:30 p.m., the power came back on. That evening, I went for a walk and saw something that amazed me: only our street had power; the rest of the neighborhood was still in the dark. God honored the words I spoke in faith.

The Bible also tells us about Joshua. He commanded the sun and moon to stand still, and they did, so the people of Israel could defeat their enemies. Creation obeyed his words.

I had a similar moment once when our family was flying from Tampa to Houston. Suddenly, the plane started shaking hard and swinging side to side. People screamed and cried. I was scared too, but at that moment, I called on the name of Jesus: "Jesus. Jesus. Jesus!" Within minutes, the plane steadied and returned to normal.

Psalm 91:15 (NKJV) says, **"He shall call upon Me, and I will answer him; I will be with him in trouble; I will deliver him and honor him."**

When you face turbulence, on a plane, in a storm, or in your life, don't be silent. Speak to the atmosphere. Declare peace. Jesus rebuked the winds, and so can you. Your words carry power!

Taming Your Tongue

James 3 clearly talks about the importance of taming our tongue. Think about Goliath, the giant Philistine who came against Israel. Every day, he mocked God and challenged the Israelites to fight. 1 Samuel 17:10 (NIV) says, **"Then the Philistine said, 'This day I defy the armies of Israel! Give me a man and let us fight each other!'"** When King Saul and the Israelites heard Goliath's words, they were terrified.

Now listen to the powerful words of David!

> 1 Samuel 17:46–47 (NIV) – "This day the Lord will deliver you into my hands, and I will strike you down and cut off your head... All those gathered here will know that it is not by sword or spear that the Lord saves; for the battle is the Lord's, and He will give all of you into our hands."

Wow, what confidence and faith! This young man used his tongue to honor and glorify the Lord. He said boldly, "I come against you in the name of the Lord Almighty, the God of the armies of Israel, whom you have defiled."

Goliath used his words to curse and mock God. But David used his mouth to declare the power and victory of God. We also face "giants" in our lives, words of fear, anxiety, shame, intimidation, or condemnation. The question is: How do we respond? Just like David, we must learn to say, "I come against this in the name of the Lord!" Our tongue can either build us up or tear us down. It can be used for good or for evil.

James 3:2 (NLT) says, **"Indeed, we all make many mistakes. For if we could control our tongues, we would be perfect and could also control ourselves in every other way."**

James compares the tongue to:

A bit in a horse's mouth is small but can control the entire animal.

A rudder on a ship is tiny, but it steers a massive vessel wherever the pilot wants it to go.

A spark is small but can set a whole forest on fire.

He says the tongue is a fire, a world of evil, corrupting the whole body, and setting the entire course of one's life on fire. He even says it's set on fire by hell itself. He adds that while humans have tamed every kind of animal, no human being can tame the tongue. It is a restless evil, full of deadly poison.

With the same tongue, we praise God, yet we also curse people, people who were made in God's image. But how do we curse someone? Sometimes it happens when we speak out of strong emotions, such as anger, frustration, or bitterness. For example, if you say, "I hate you," in a moment of rage, that phrase cuts deeply. It can make someone feel worthless, unloved, and rejected, and even cause them to lash back in anger. You may hear, "Well, I hate you too!"

Proverbs 12:18 (NIV) says, **"The words of the reckless pierce like a sword, but the tongue of the wise brings healing."**

Proverbs 15:1(NIV) reminds us, **"A gentle answer turns away wrath, but a harsh word stirs up anger."**

On the other hand, when you tell someone "I love you" in a soft, caring tone, it can heal and uplift them. They feel cherished, valued, and grateful, and more often than not, they respond, "I love you too."

Proverbs 16:24 (NKJV) says, **"Pleasant words are like a honeycomb, sweetness to the soul and health to the bones."**

How Can You Tame Your Tongue?

Surrender your heart and your tongue to the Lord.

Ask God for grace to control your speech. You can't do it with your own strength.

Say this prayer every day. Psalm 19:14 (NKJV) – **"Let the words of my mouth and the meditation of my heart be acceptable in your sight, O Lord, my strength and my Redeemer."**

> Psalm 39:1 (NIV) – "I said, 'I will watch my ways and keep my tongue from sin; I will put a muzzle on my mouth while in the presence of the wicked.'"

Align your heart with the Spirit of God. Let His peace and truth guide your thoughts and words. Meditate on Scriptures about the power of the tongue. James Chapter 3 is full of insight, reminding us how a single spark (your words) can destroy or build a life.

In the book of Acts, we see how tongues of fire rested on believers in the upper room. That Holy Spirit fire gave them the courage to speak truth boldly. Peter spoke, and people from many nations understood him in their languages. The fire of the Spirit gave power to their tongues.

Ask for forgiveness for any hurtful or unloving words.

> Ephesians 4:31–32 (NIV) – "Get rid of all bitterness, rage, and anger, brawling, and slander, along with every form of malice. Be kind and compassionate to one another, forgiving each other, just as in Christ God forgave you."

Choose to use your words to build and bless others. Let your tongue be used for encouragement, not destruction.

> Colossians 4:6 (NIV) – "Let your conversation be always full of grace, seasoned with salt, so that you may know how to answer everyone."

If words hold the power to create, then every sentence we speak becomes a brushstroke on the canvas of reality. We are never merely talking; we are shaping. The question is not whether our words have power, but what kind of power they release.

As you've seen in this chapter, God has entrusted you with the ability to speak life. So, guard your mouth, align your words with His truth, and boldly declare His promises. Let your tongue become a vessel of His power, creating a life that reflects His glory.

To speak in alignment with God's creative force is to become conscious of what flows from your mouth. Creation responds to conviction. Heaven responds to faith. Words backed by belief carry a vibration that moves unseen realms. When our speech harmonizes with divine truth, our words cease to be noise; they become instruments of creation.

Jesus demonstrated this perfectly. He spoke to storms, and they were still. He spoke to the dead, and they rose. He blessed the bread, and it multiplied. His words carried authority because they were perfectly aligned with the Father's will. He said, "The words I speak to you are spirit, and they are life."

That same potential rests within us. We are called to speak with purpose to let our words reflect heaven's rhythm, not earth's fear. When you speak, let there be light instead of darkness, peace instead of chaos, healing instead of despair, you echo that original command: "Let there be."

When faith fuels your words, they carry energy beyond your own. Heaven partners with your voice. What you declare in alignment with God's purpose begins to shape what is unseen until it becomes visible. This is not super-stition or wishful thinking; it is the echo of Genesis, still resonating in human speech.

Reflection Questions:

1. Do you genuinely believe that your words carry creative power? What do your daily conversations say about what you believe?

2. When faced with sickness or weakness, what is your first response? Do you speak about healing and life, or do you give more voice to fear and symptoms?

3. Have you ever spoken negatively about your finan-cial situation? How can you begin to speak faith and provision based on God's promises instead?

4. In what areas of your life do you need to take author-ity and speak God's Word with boldness? (Health, finances, relationships, storms of life, emotional battles?)

5. Have you used your tongue to hurt others or speak words that don't honor God? What steps can you

take to tame your tongue and speak words that bring healing and encouragement?

6. Are you regularly declaring God's Word over your life? If not, what Scriptures can you start confessing daily to build your faith?

7. Like David before Goliath, do you use your words to glorify God in the face of life's challenges? What "giants" do you need to confront with faith-filled declarations?

8. Have you surrendered your tongue to the Lord? What might change in your life if you did?

Closing Prayer

Heavenly Father,

We thank You for the gift of Your Word and for revealing to us the incredible power You have placed in our tongues. You spoke creation into existence, and You've made us in Your image and called us to speak life, healing, hope, and truth. Lord, forgive us for the times we've used our words to doubt, to curse, or to tear down. Today, we surrender our tongues to You. Cleanse our lips, purify our hearts, and let every word that proceeds from our mouths bring glory to Your name.

Father, teach us to declare Your promises over our health, our finances, our families, and even the storms we face. May we speak with the authority of sons and daughters of the Most High God, knowing that when we align our words with Your truth, mountains move, healing comes, and peace reigns.

Holy Spirit, fill our mouths with wisdom and our hearts with boldness. Let us be like David, who faced giants not with fear, but with declarations of Your power. Let us be like Jesus, who calmed the storm with a word. Let our tongues be instruments of revival, speaking grace, truth, and power into every dry and weary place in our lives and in the lives of others.

We declare today that our tongues will be used to bless and not curse. We will speak to our bodies and say, "Be healed in Jesus' name." We will speak to our finances and say, "My God shall supply all my needs." We will speak to the storms and say, "Peace, be still." And we will speak to our future and say, "The Lord is making a way where there seems to be no way."

Let the words of our mouths and the meditations of our hearts be acceptable in Your sight, O Lord, our Rock, and our Redeemer.

We seal this prayer in the mighty and matchless name of Jesus.

Amen.

www.ingramcontent.com/pod-product-compliance
Lightning Source LLC
Chambersburg PA
CBHW051543050726
47595CB00002B/607